THE ARCHBISHOPS
of CANTERBURY

A Tale of Church and State

John Butler

T0347137

Acknowledgements and Sources

I am grateful to Chris Needham for inviting me to write the text for this book, and to Susan Swalwell, Abigail Wood, Claire Handy and Sophie Nickelson for their expertise in seeing the project through to completion. My grateful thanks also go to friends and colleagues in Canterbury whose contributions to the book have been invaluable: Ivy Calvino, Toby Huitson, Richard Llewellin, Leonie Seliger, Fred Whitemore and Cressida Williams. They bear no responsibility for any errors.

The material in this book has been drawn from the following sources. As far as possible, major facts have been checked across more than one source. Any errors are the sole responsibility of the author.

Bede. *Ecclesiastical History of the English People*, London: Penguin Books, revised edition, 1990

Bevan, G.M. ed. *Portraits of the Archbishops of Canterbury*, London: A. R. Mowbray & Co Ltd., 1908

Brooks, N. *The Early History of the Church of Canterbury*, London and New York: Leicester University Press, 1984

Cannon, J. and Griffiths, R. *The Oxford Illustrated History of the British Monarchy*, Oxford: Oxford University Press, 1988

Carpenter, E. *Cantuar: The Archbishops in their Office*, London: A. R. Mowbray & Co Ltd., 1988

Collinson, P., Ramsay, N., and Sparks, M. eds. *A History of Canterbury Cathedral*, Oxford: Oxford University Press, 1995

Ingram Hill, D. *Canterbury Cathedral*, London: Bell & Hyman Ltd., 1986

Matthew, H.G.C. and Harrison, B. eds. *Oxford Dictionary of National Biography. From the Earliest Times to the Year 2000*, Oxford: Oxford University Press, revised edition, 2004

Maxwell-Stuart, P.G *The Archbishops of Canterbury*, Stroud, Gloucestershire: Tempus Publishing Ltd., 2006

Powicke, F.M. and Fryde, E. B. *Handbook of British Chronology*, London: Offices of the Royal Historical Society, 1961

Stanley, A.P. *Historical Memorials of Canterbury*, London: John Murray, 1912

Swanton, M. tr. and ed. *The Anglo-Saxon Chronicles*, London: Phoenix Press, 2000

Wikimedia Foundation Inc. *Wikipedia: The Free Encyclopaedia*, articles on named archbishops of Canterbury

Woodruff, C.E. and Danks, W. *Memorials of the Cathedral and Priory of Christ in Canterbury*, London: Chapman and Hall Ltd, 1912

CONTENTS

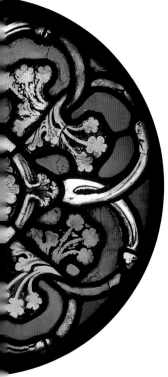

INTRODUCTION

The archbishopric of Canterbury is the oldest continuous institution in Britain – older than the English crown and much older than Parliament. The first archbishop, Augustine, took up office in 597, a mere two centuries after the Romans had left, and since then his successors have survived the demise of the early Anglo-Saxon kingdoms, the emergence of the English nation, the Norman Conquest, the Protestant Reformation, the English Civil War, the evolution of parliamentary democracy, the importation of foreign kings, the rise of modern science, the Industrial Revolution, two World Wars, the rapid growth of cultural pluralism and, in recent times, a marked decline in formal religious observance. Although there have been occasional gaps in the line of succession – most notably between 1645 and 1660 when the monarchy was in exile and the Church of England went into hibernation – the acknowledged leader of the English Church has, from very early times, been the Bishop of the diocese of Canterbury, a small market town in Kent on the southern-eastern edge of England. He – for there have so far been no women – is graced with the title of Lord Archbishop of Canterbury, Primate of All England.

The following pages recount how this ancient and venerable institution has shaped and been shaped by the social, political and religious events that have sculpted the contours of British history for a millennium and a half. It is a story of faith and power, wisdom and folly, leadership and timidity, high principle and craven self-interest. At its heart is a profound tension that has engaged the minds and spirits of those who have followed in Augustine's footsteps – a tension between, on the one hand, a responsibility to proclaim the gospel and lead the Church and, on the other, an obligation to serve the interests of the state and its rulers. The nature and intensity of the tension have varied from one historical period to another, but few of the hundred or so archbishops of Canterbury since Augustine have remained entirely immune from problems created by these dual loyalties.

In the early years of Anglo-Saxon Britain, the archbishops were heavily dependent on the goodwill of the feudal – and feuding – kings of Kent, Mercia and Wessex, but by the end of the first millennium, a more equal and productive relationship had begun to be forged between monarch and primate. Dunstan's fruitful collaboration with King Edgar the Peaceful in the 960s and 970s gave England an era of almost unprecedented peace and prosperity, and Lanfranc's partnership with William the Conqueror was equally effective in establishing Norman rule in the country from 1066 onwards.

By the early Middle Ages, archbishops had come to be valued as much for their administrative and diplomatic skills as for their spiritual qualities and many of them held high offices of state under the crown. Hubert Walter, who was Archbishop of Canterbury from 1193 to 1205, accompanied Richard Lionheart on the third crusade to the Holy Land and negotiated the peace treaty with Saladin that gave Christians access to the Holy Sepulchre in Jerusalem; even as late as the 17th century, William Juxon, archbishop from 1660 to 1663, doubled up as First Lord of the Admiralty. From very early times, moreover, it has been the archbishops of Canterbury who have crowned the kings and queens of England, and even today the archbishop is the senior non-royal citizen of the United Kingdom.

RIGHT: Victorian decorative border, Canterbury Cathedral

Yet the occupants of St Augustine's throne have often found themselves treading a fine line, for the interests of the State have not always coincided with those of the Church, and many archbishops have been able to proclaim the gospel and lead the Church only by defying the monarch or challenging parliament. Some have paid a high price. Thomas Becket, who gave himself up to martyrdom in 1170 in defence of the early medieval church against an overbearing king, is far from alone in having suffered at the hands of secular powers. He is not even unique in having paid the ultimate price: in 1012, Alphege was brutally murdered at Greenwich by Viking invaders; in 1556 Thomas Cranmer was burnt at the stake in Oxford on the orders of the Catholic Mary Tudor, and as late as 1645, William Laud was executed on Tower Hill at the behest of the Long Parliament. In the modern era, of course, such drastic penalties are no longer exacted, but archbishops speaking in the name of the Church can – and do – still challenge the legislative intentions of parliament through their voice in the House of Lords, and they can – and do – still incur the wrath of prime ministers, as Robert Runcie discovered at the hands of Margaret Thatcher in the 1980s. It is an enduring paradox that, while the archbishopric of Canterbury sits at the pinnacle of the British establishment, its incumbents have sometimes been among the fiercest critics of establishment values and interests.

Yet it could fairly be said that the very existence of the paradox is a sign of the health of the Church, for Christianity has always championed the poor and the disadvantaged against the interests of the rich and the powerful. If the time ever came when an archbishop of Canterbury felt unable to speak out on behalf of the Church or to criticise the ruling powers of the day, even at the risk of upsetting those in very high places, something of inestimable value in the history of the English people would have been lost. Happily, such a day is not in prospect.

THE GREGORIAN MISSION: 597–653

By the time Augustine and his fellow monks landed near Ramsgate in AD597 on a mission from Pope Gregory the Great to bring Roman Christianity to southern Britain, much of the country had long been converted to other varieties of the faith. In the north and west, a form of Christianity – known loosely as Celtic Christianity – had moved in through Brittany, Cornwall and Ireland. It was typically organised around simple churches and small communities of monks distinguished by their iconic tonsures and hermit-like lifestyles. In the south and east of Britain, the existence of a different form of early Christianity is evidenced in stories such as that of Alban, a pagan who converted to Christianity after sheltering a priest in his house.

These early Christian communities were doubtless encouraged by the adoption of Christianity as the official religion of the Roman Empire following the conversion of the Emperor Constantine in 313, and their faith survived not only the departure of the Romans from Britain in about 400 but also the subsequent arrival of Anglo-Saxon invaders from northern Europe. In time, the Germanic cultures of these immigrant peoples intermingled with local traditions and customs, preserving a good deal of the religious legacy left behind by the departing Romans.

It was against this background that the Gregorian mission to Britain set forth, headed by a rather inexperienced monk from Rome, Augustine. He brought with him a sixth-century copy of the gospels, now known as the Gospels of St Augustine, which is still used at the enthronement of new archbishops of Canterbury. Landing on the Kentish coast at Ebbsfleet, Augustine and a few dozen other monks and lay clerks were received by Ethelbert, the king of Kent and the feudal overlord of the Anglo-Saxon kingdoms south of the River Humber. Although Ethelbert was not himself a Christian when the missionaries arrived, he gave them house-room in Canterbury and allowed them to preach – a decision that was doubtless influenced by his wife Bertha, a Christian princess from Paris who, upon her marriage to King Ethelbert, had been allowed to continue practising her faith.

Pope Gregory had expected Augustine to set up his base in London, but he never got any further than Canterbury, judging it wiser to settle in a hospitable location close to Gaul. He began work on a cathedral in Canterbury, possibly on the site of a former Roman temple, and he founded a monastery, dedicated to St Peter and St Paul, just to the east of the city walls. Later renamed St Augustine's Abbey after its founder, it became the burial site of many of the early archbishops, including Augustine himself. When further missionaries arrived from Rome in 601, they brought with them a pallium, the papal insignia of an archbishop that confirmed the legitimacy of Augustine and all his successors up to the Reformation in the 16th century.

Following his death in 604, Augustine was succeeded as archbishop by Laurence, who had been part of the original mission in 597 and who had later been sent back to Rome to seek Pope Gregory's responses to a number of questions to which Augustine wanted answers. Laurence followed Augustine's policy of consolidation in Kent, but he suffered a setback when King Ethelbert's son and successor, Edbald, reverted to paganism and withdrew much of the

RIGHT: St Augustine, Canterbury Cathedral, Cloister, 20th century

8

support that his father had given. Disheartened, Laurence contemplated a return to Rome, but he experienced a vivid dream in which he was berated by St Peter for his timidity and woke to find his body scourged as if by a whip. King Edbald was so impressed by Laurence's dream that he immediately converted to Christianity and was baptised into the faith. Thereafter, life was much easier for the fledgling Roman Church in England.

Laurence died in 619 and was succeeded first by Mellitus and then by Justus. Mellitus was among the second wave of missionaries sent by Pope Gregory, arriving in Canterbury in 601 laden with books and artefacts needed for the furtherance of the mission. A Roman of noble birth, Mellitus was consecrated as the first Bishop of London in 604 but was quickly expelled by the pagan sons of Saeberht, the Christian king of the East Saxons, following their father's death in about 616. In 619, however, Mellitus followed Laurence as Archbishop of Canterbury. He suffered badly from gout, an affliction that also plagued many of his successors, but that did not prevent him from saving Canterbury when an all-engulfing fire threatened it. Ordering his servants to carry him into the path of the flames, his prayers for deliverance were answered as the wind suddenly swung to the north and the fire subsided.

When Mellitus's successor, Justus, died in 627 he was succeeded by Honorius, the last of the Roman missionaries to become Archbishop of Canterbury. During his twenty-five years in office, Honorius encouraged the spread of Roman Christianity beyond the south-east corner of Britain. He sent a Burgundian priest, Felix, to evangelise among the subjects of King Sigebert in East Anglia, and he lived to see the burgeoning success of Aidan in Northumbria. It was during Honorius's time that a young Northumbrian nobleman, Wilfrid – later to become one of the great northern saints – passed through Canterbury on his way to Rome. Three centuries later, in 948, one of Honorius's successors as archbishop, Oda, seized the relics of St Wilfrid from Ripon and brought them to Canterbury where they remained until the purges of Henry VIII in 1538. When Honorius died in 653, it was time for the locals to take over.

ABOVE: **Pope Gregory the Great, Canterbury Cathedral, Cloister, 20th century**

RIGHT: **King Ethelbert, Canterbury Cathedral, Chapter House, 19th century**

FAR RIGHT: **Queen Bertha, Canterbury Cathedral, Chapter House, 19th century**

King Ethelbert ✣ ✣ Queen Bertha

THE ANGLO-SAXON SUCCESSION: 653–805

After five Roman occupants of the Archbishop's Throne (Augustine, Laurence, Mellitus, Justus and Honorius), the sixth was a native Saxon, Frithona, who changed his name at the time of his consecration in 655 to Deusdedit ('God has given'). He was the first in a long line of English archbishops of Canterbury that was broken only by his immediate successor, Theodore. Deusdedit's period of office is not well documented, and the archiepiscopal throne remained vacant for four years after his death. The most important religious event in England at the time was the great Synod of Whitby in 664, but Deusdedit was not among those who attended. It was summoned at the behest of Hilda, the founding abbess of the eponymous monastery at Whitby, and was intended to sort out the disagreements that had arisen between the Celtic churches north of the Humber and the Roman Church in the south. The outcome broadly favoured the south, bringing the Northumbrian Church largely into line with Roman practices. The Pope was confirmed as the rock on which the English Church should be built, and the seat of the Bishop of Northumbria was moved from Lindisfarne to York. The effect was to strengthen the authority of Canterbury over the development of Christianity throughout the whole of England.

Deusdedit did not live to enjoy the fruits of Whitby, for he died of the plague in July 664; but his successor, Theodore, took full advantage of Canterbury's burgeoning supremacy over the north. He is generally regarded as the first archbishop to command the obedience of the whole of Anglo-Saxon Christianity, making him arguably the most influential churchman in England between Augustine and Dunstan, three hundred years later. A native of Tarsus in Cilicia, Theodore was a Roman monk when he was appointed to the see of Canterbury after the previous candidate, Wighard, had died in Rome before he could collect the pallium. Arriving in Canterbury in 669, Theodore set about imposing order on the English Church, creating new sees and consecrating bishops to fill them. It brought him into conflict with Wilfrid, now the Bishop of York, when he tried to divide the see of York into four smaller, more manageable parts. Wilfrid objected to the plan and appealed to Pope Agatho who upheld his complaint, but Theodore nevertheless went ahead.

Theodore's greatest achievement as archbishop was his enlightened promotion of learning. A man of catholic interests and wide scholarship, the school that he founded at Canterbury was highly unusual in the Roman Church in favouring the Greek fathers over their Latin counterparts and in elevating literal interpretations of the Bible above allegorical ones. The school also taught Roman law, rules for the composition of Latin poetry, music and biblical exposition. Theodore died in Canterbury in 690 at the age of nearly ninety and was buried close to Augustine in the abbey church of St Peter and St Paul, a short distance to the east of the cathedral.

Theodore was a hard act to follow, and none of his Anglo-Saxon successors for the next three hundred or so years managed to emulate him. After Theodore came Berhtwald, archbishop from 693 to 731, who was Abbot of the monastery of St Mary at Reculver on the north Kent coast before being promoted to Canterbury. An ally of King Wihtred of Kent, Berhtwald spent much

RIGHT: St Denis wearing the papal pallium, Canterbury Cathedral, northwest transept, 15th century

FAR RIGHT: St Wilfred, Canterbury Cathedral, northwest transept, 15th century

of his time in office trying to resolve the continuing controversy over Wilfrid's position in York. The issue was finally settled at the Council of Austerfield in 702 when Wilfrid was persuaded to resign the bishopric of York and return to his monastery in Ripon. He was reconciled to Berhtwald at the Council of Nidd in 705 and died a few years later.

After Berhtwald came Tatwin (731–734), a monk from the kingdom of Mercia renowned principally for the riddles that he compiled in the form of acrostics on such diverse topics as charity, the five senses, the alphabet, scissors, anvils and swords. Next was Nothelm (735–739), another Mercian, who received the pallium from Pope Gregory III in 736 and continued to develop the administrative structure of the Church by rearranging the sees in Mercia. Nothelm corresponded with Bede and supplied him with some of the material for his *Ecclesiastical History of the English People* – for which Bede, in the preface to his great work, was duly grateful.

Nothelm was succeeded by Cuthbert (739–760), a monk of noble birth whose principal action as archbishop was to reverse the earlier decision by Theodore and recreate York as a single see with its own archbishop, Ecgbert. At Canterbury, Cuthbert built a chapel at the south-east corner of the cathedral, dedicated to St John the Baptist, to serve both as a baptistery and a mausoleum to house the tombs of himself and his successors. This probably marked the end of the usual practice of archbishops being buried in the abbey church of St Peter and St Paul, and Cuthbert himself was the first to be interred in his new chapel.

The next archbishops after Cuthbert were Bregowine (761–764) and Jaenberht (765–792). Very little contemporary information has survived about Bregowine, but with the consecration of Jaenberht, the tensions between Church and monarchy came once more to the fore. Kent was now under the over-lordship of King Offa of Mercia, a powerful Christian monarch who appointed Jaenberht to Canterbury and secured the pallium for him; but in 776 a Kentish rebellion, culminating in the Battle of Otford, temporarily secured Kent's freedom from Offa's control. It is possible that Jaenberht was involved in the uprising in some way, for thereafter his relationship with Offa deteriorated, and in 787 the King successfully persuaded Pope Adrian I to divide the province of Canterbury into two by creating a new metropolitan see of Lichfield with its own archbishop, Hyberht.

The rival see did not last for long, for Jaenberht's successor Ethelhard – who was consecrated by Archbishop Hyberht of Lichfield in 793 – eventually managed to secure its dissolution, but not before things took another violent turn. When King Offa died in 796, the control of Kent was seized back from Mercia by King Eadberht of Kent, who turned on Archbishop Ethelhard and forced him out of office.

Kent, though, was soon retaken by Offa's successor, King Coenwulf, and Ethelhard was restored to Canterbury, where he set about reclaiming the province's possessions that had been ceded to Lichfield. Hyberht naturally contested Ethelhard's claims, but Ethelhard pressed them home in 802 by visiting Pope Leo III in Rome. At the Council of Clovesho in the following year, it was decreed that the rival metropolitan see of Lichfield should never have been established in the first place and that Canterbury should henceforth be the only southern province.

Other threats were now looming, however. Ten years before the Council of Clovesho, in 793, Viking raiders had ransacked the monastery at Lindisfarne, thus beginning a long period of Norse engagement in Britain. It was to change the religious face of the country.

THE ARRIVAL OF
THE VIKINGS: 805–959

When Ethelhard died in 805, he was followed as archbishop by Wulfred, formerly the archdeacon of Canterbury. Wulfred, who came from a wealthy family in what is now Middlesex, devoted much of his time as archbishop to reforming the life of the non-monastic clergy of the cathedral. He required them to eat together, to give their personal property to the chapter – the cathedral's governing body – and to conform to the strict demands of the liturgy. Wulfred did not, however, enjoy a harmonious relationship with King Coenwulf of Mercia, disputing the King's control over the monasteries and omitting his image from the coins that were struck in the archbishop's name. Coenwulf retaliated by depriving Wulfred of his office; but by 822 he was once more officiating as archbishop when he crowned Coenwulf's successor, his brother Ceolwulf, as King of Mercia. Thereafter relations between King and Archbishop improved.

Wulfred's successor as archbishop, Feologild, was in office for less than three months in 832 when he died and was replaced by Ceolnoth. Much of Ceolnoth's time was spent coping with attacks by Viking raiders, who he tried to buy off by minting his own coins. He also had to develop a working relationship with the royal house of Wessex, which had wrested the control of Kent from Mercia following the Battle of Ellandun near Swindon, in 825. At a council held at Kingston-upon-Thames in 838, Ceolnoth entered into an alliance with King Egbert of Wessex in which, in return for his protection against the Vikings, Egbert was acknowledged as the secular patron of the Kentish monasteries. The King was, however, powerless to prevent the closure of several monasteries in Kent when they were ransacked by Viking marauders who were over-wintering on the Isle of Sheppey in 851 and the Isle of Thanet in 855.

When Ceolnoth died in 870, he was succeeded first by Ethelred (870–888) and then by Plegmund (890–c.923). Archbishop Ethelred, like his predecessor, was much troubled by Viking invaders passing through Kent, though it seems that large numbers of Danes were converted to Christianity during his time in office. Ethelred also clashed with the King of Wessex, Alfred the Great, over the extent of royal interference in ecclesiastical affairs. Ethelred even wrote to Pope John VIII complaining about Alfred's behaviour. The Pope's reply assured the Archbishop that Canterbury continued to enjoy the full support of Rome and that he had written to the King urging him to respect the rights of the Church. Some have seen the correspondence as evidence of an ecclesiastic plot against Alfred, but of this there is no definitive proof.

Ethelred's successor, Plegmund – who was consecrated in 890 after a gap of two years – seems to have enjoyed a better relationship with King Alfred, who not only appointed him archbishop but also summoned him to his court in Winchester. There, Plegmund joined a group of scholars translating Pope Gregory the Great's masterpiece, *Pastoral Rule*, from the original Latin into Old English. The treatise, which was one of the most influential works of early western Christendom, had first been brought to Britain by Augustine in 597, and the Winchester translation, done in the 890s, is among the oldest known books in English. King Alfred saw the project as part of a

RIGHT: Viking raiders began to invade the shores of Britain in the 8th century

wider plan to improve the standard of scholarship throughout his realm, and Plegmund's successful involvement in the enterprise gave him the impetus to do the same in the Church. He greatly improved the linguistic and calligraphic competency of scribes in the monasteries, and he ensured that every shire in Wessex had its own bishop to promote learning and scholarship.

Plegmund died in about 923 and was succeeded by Athelm, a Saxon monk who began his career at Glastonbury and who came to Canterbury from the bishopric of Wells. Little is known of Athelm's short time as archbishop, though he probably crowned Alfred the Great's grandson, Athelstan, as king of the Anglo-Saxons in 924. Athelm died in 926 and was buried in the chapel of St John the Baptist, to the south-east of the cathedral, that had been built by Archbishop Cuthbert some two hundred years earlier. However, his body, together with those of several other early archbishops, was later exhumed and reinterred in the Norman cathedral that was built in the 1070s by Archbishop Lanfranc.

The next archbishop, Wulfhelm, was a frequent attender at the court of King Athelstan where he became almost the monarch's right-hand man. Wulfhelm advised Athelstan on the revision of England's legal codes and he was instrumental in arranging the marriage of the King's sister, Ethel, to the future Holy Roman Emperor, Otto the Great.

ABOVE: Viking invaders land on the south coast of England, destroying a Saxon church

When Wulfhelm died in 941 he was succeeded by Oda, the son of a Danish invader who had probably been introduced to Christianity through his adoption by a pious English nobleman, Ethelhelm. In 956 Oda crowned the raucous teenager Eadwig who ruled as king of the Anglo-Saxons until his premature death in 959. Eadwig's short reign was tarnished by disputes with his nobles and senior figures in the Church. Archbishop Oda was one of the first to experience the young King's wrath after the Archbishop chastised Eadwig for abandoning his coronation banquet to cavort with a noblewoman and her daughter.

In maiorem Dei gloriam et in piam memoriam

At Canterbury, Oda carried out an extensive reconstruction of the Saxon cathedral, raising the walls, adding aisles to the nave and building towers on the north and south sides. In order not to disrupt the services while the work was in progress, Oda prayed that no rain should fall on the roofless cathedral – and tradition has it that his prayers were answered. Although there were many storms during the three years that the work took, they all carefully skirted round the building, leaving the worshippers dry.

Oda's nominated successor in 958 was the Bishop of Winchester, Elfsige, who unfortunately died on a visit to Rome before his installation. He was replaced by Byrhthelm, the Bishop of Dorset; but he fared little better than Elfsige, being dismissed for incompetence before he could take up office. Both Elfsige and Byrhthelm had been chosen by the unruly King Eadwig and neither is counted in the conventional list of archbishops of Canterbury. At this point the future of the archbishopric may have seemed uncertain, but when Eadwig died in mysterious circumstances in 959 he was succeeded as king by his younger brother, Edgar the Peaceful, who promptly appointed one of his late brother's bitterest enemies to be the new Archbishop of Canterbury: Dunstan. It was an appointment that changed the face of English Christianity.

LEFT: Oda prays for rain to desist during the rebuilding of the cathedral, Canterbury Cathedral, Nave, 19th century

THE REVIVAL OF MONASTICISM: 959–1005

Saint Dunstan is a towering figure – not only in the history of the Church in England but of England itself. It has been said of him that if the 10th century gave shape to English history, Dunstan gave shape to the 10th century. He was born into a noble family in Somerset in 909 and studied as a boy under Irish monks at Glastonbury. After time spent at the court of King Athelstan, Dunstan was installed as Abbot of Glastonbury where he set about restoring a monastic form of life based on the rule of St Benedict, which had been all but extinguished in England under pressure from the Vikings. With the accession of King Eadred to the Anglo-Saxon throne in 946, Dunstan was recalled to court, but when Eadred was succeeded by the loutish King Eadwig in 956, he immediately fell out with the young monarch and was forced into exile in Flanders.

Dunstan's fortunes changed when Eadwig died suddenly in 959 and was succeeded by his brother, King Edgar the Peaceful, who recalled Dunstan from exile and appointed him Archbishop of Canterbury. Thus began a fruitful collaboration between King and Archbishop that breathed new life into the English Church and transformed the archbishopric into a political force in the land. Dunstan presided over the coronation of King Edgar at Bath in 959 and later of King Eadweard the Martyr in 975 and King Ethelred the Unready in 978. The liturgy that he devised for these three ceremonies still finds a place in Britain's coronation rites.

Dunstan is celebrated above all for rescuing English monasticism from the doldrums into which it had sunk. During his almost thirty years as archbishop, new monasteries were built, and at some of the great cathedrals, including Canterbury, monks began replacing the secular canons (priests who were members of the cathedral chapter but were not monks). Those who remained as canons were increasingly required to live by monastic rules and were even encouraged to take vows of celibacy. Under Dunstan, too, the liturgy was reformed and prayers for the royal family were included for the first time.

As part of his monastic reforms, Dunstan insisted that every monk should have a craftwork skill. Metalwork seems to have been particularly favoured, and Dunstan is often depicted tweaking the devil's nose with a pair of tongs. The story was preserved in a popular folk song:

'St Dunstan, as the story goes, once pulled the devil by the nose with red-hot tongs, which made him roar, that he was heard three miles or more.'

Dunstan's reforms were not, however, confined to the cathedrals and monasteries: in the parishes, the practice of simony (the selling of ecclesiastical offices for money) was outlawed, and the nepotism that had allowed parish priests to appoint their relatives to positions under their patronage was curtailed. The country, too, benefited from Dunstan's conscientious influence in court circles. Law and order was tightened up throughout the realm, trained bands of vigilantes operated in a number of places, and a rudimentary navy guarded the shores from Viking raiders. Under King Edgar and Archbishop Dunstan, England enjoyed a level of peace unknown in living memory.

RIGHT: St Dunstan delivers King Eadwig from Hell, Canterbury Cathedral, Choir, 12th century

ORII

Dunstan's influence at court ended with the coronation of King Ethelred the Unready in 978 and he returned to Canterbury for the last ten years of his life. He became devoted to the Canterbury saints and spent long hours in prayer at their shrines. In his sermon on Ascension Day in 988, Dunstan announced his impending death. That afternoon, he chose the spot for his tomb and went to his bed, never to rise from it again.

After such a stellar archiepiscopate, there was bound to be something of an anti-climax, and the three archbishops who succeeded Dunstan have largely languished in his shadow. Ethelgar, a former monk at Glastonbury and Winchester, was installed in 988, but he was archbishop for less than two years. His successor, Sigeric the Serious, was Bishop of Ramsbury before receiving the pallium in Rome in about 990. Sigeric is remembered principally for his part in paying tribute money to the Vikings. In 991 he advised King Ethelred the Unready to pay ten thousand pounds of silver to the Danish king, Sweyn Forkbeard. It resulted in a temporary cessation of Forkbeard's rampages through the country, but when the Viking returned for more, the money had to be raised through a debilitating tax known as Danegeld. In 994 Sigeric paid his own tribute money to the Danes to prevent Canterbury Cathedral from being attacked.

After Sigeric came Elfric of Abingdon, who continued to hold the bishopric of Ramsbury throughout his ten years as archbishop. There is a tradition that prior to his election, Elfric had supported Dunstan's policy of replacing the secular canons of the cathedral with monks. Alarmed by this, the Canterbury chapter made representations to Rome that Elfric should not be appointed archbishop. However, Pope Gregory V insisted that only a candidate who had royal support should get the job. When Elfric himself arrived in Rome in 997, he received the pallium directly from the Pope's hand. He died in 1005 and was followed by Canterbury's first martyred archbishop, Alphege.

MARTYRDOM AND CONQUEST: 1005–1070

Saint Alphege was the first of five archbishops of Canterbury to die a violent death. An austere and pious west-country monk, Alphege became Bishop of Winchester in 984 and was commissioned by King Ethelred the Unready to meet King Olaf Tryggvason of Norway to buy off his raids on London and Wessex. Tribute money was duly paid, but in the process, Olaf converted to Christianity and promised that he would never again come to England 'with warlike intent' – a promise that he seemingly kept.

Alphege was installed as Archbishop of Canterbury in 1005 and received the pallium from Pope John VIII in Rome. Once in office, Alphege was plagued by marauding bands of Danish invaders who, impervious to the tribute money that was offered to them, rampaged through the south of England. In September 1011, a Danish force besieged Canterbury and the city surrendered. Alphege was captured and held to ransom for £3,000, but he forbade the Church to pay it. Incensed by the Archbishop's obstinacy, the Danes brought him before a quasi-legal court meeting in Greenwich at Easter 1012, and there he was pelted with bones and cattle skulls before being struck on the head with the butt of an axe. Mortally wounded, the Archbishop sank down and, in the words of the *Anglo-Saxon Chronicle*, 'his holy blood fell on the earth and sent forth his holy soul to God's kingdom'.

Alphege was buried initially at St Paul's in London, but with the consent of King Cnut his body was returned to Canterbury in 1023 and reinterred in the cathedral on the north side of the high altar. It may still be there. A later archbishop, Anselm, declared Alphege to have been a true martyr for justice; and when Thomas Becket faced his own imminent death in 1170, it was to St Alphege as well as to God that he commended his soul.

Alphege was succeeded in 1013 by Lyfing, who was appointed to Canterbury by King Ethelred the Unready. He was enthroned by the Archbishop of York, Wulfstan. Like Alphege before him, Lyfing was captured by Danish invaders but was released (without, in his case, any record of a ransom having been demanded) in time to attend the Witan, an Anglo-Saxon version of the Privy Council, in 1014. He later crowned King Edmund Ironside in 1016 and King Cnut (the son of Sweyn Forkbeard) in the following year. Lyfing died in 1020 and was buried in Canterbury Cathedral, the building that he had begun to restore after its partial destruction by the Danes. The *Anglo-Saxon Chronicle* described him as 'a sagacious man, both before God and before the world'.

Lyfing was succeeded by Ethelnoth, a monk of Glastonbury who was baptised by Dunstan during his time there as abbot. The story persisted at Glastonbury that, as Ethelnoth was being baptised, his hands made a motion akin to that of a priest blessing his flock, whereupon Dunstan prophesied that he would become an archbishop. Ethelnoth was Dean of Canterbury when he was promoted by King Cnut, and, like Lyfing before him, he was enthroned by Wulfstan, Archbishop of York, in November 1020. He received the pallium in Rome from Pope Benedict VIII, bringing back with him a relic of St Augustine of Hippo. Throughout his time

RIGHT: St Alphege captured by the Danes and being transported to Greenwich in 1012, Canterbury Cathedral, Choir, 12th century

as archbishop, Ethelnoth worked closely with King Cnut, one of the most enlightened rulers of Anglo-Saxon England. He is said to have demonstrated his loyalty to the King by refusing to crown his son, Harold Harefoot, as king in 1035 because of a promise he had made that he would only crown a child born to Cnut's second wife, Queen Emma. Ethelnoth died in 1038. Some wished to revere him as a saint, but there is no evidence of any cult becoming attached to his name.

The next Archbishop of Canterbury was Eadsige, a chaplain to Cnut before his installation in 1038. Two years later he was appointed by Pope Benedict IX in Rome. In April 1043 Eadsige crowned King Edward the Confessor, the last king of Wessex, in Winchester Cathedral. In the following year, he began a four-year break from office for reasons of ill health. He died in 1050, still in office as archbishop, two years after returning to his duties.

Eadsige was succeeded first by Robert de Jumièges (archbishop for eighteen months between 1051 and 1052) and then by Stigand (1052–1070). Robert was the first of several Norman Archbishops of Canterbury, having previously been the Prior of the Abbey of St Ouen at Rouen. A friend and advisor to Edward the Confessor, he was appointed by the King first to the see of London and then to Canterbury. He was not, however, the choice of the Canterbury monks who favoured one of their own number, Ethelric, but their wishes were overruled by Edward.

Robert's short period as archbishop was dominated by his strained relationship with Godwin, the Earl of Wessex, from whom he tried to reclaim Church land and property that had been illegally appropriated. Godwin eventually persuaded Edward the Confessor to declare Robert an outlaw, and he was dismissed from Canterbury. He went into exile in 1052 and died in Normandy a few years later. Robert's treatment at the hands of the King is thought by some historians to have been a factor in the decision of William, Duke of Normandy, to invade England in 1066.

Following Robert de Jumièges's exile in 1052, Edward appointed the Bishop of Winchester, Stigand, to be his successor as archbishop. A seasoned politician, Stigand was the first non-monk to be appointed to Canterbury for nearly a hundred years, but it was an appointment that Pope Alexander II refused to recognise – partly because Stigand held the office concurrently with the bishopric of Winchester (the offence of pluralism) and partly because Robert de Jumièges, who was still alive in exile, was regarded by Alexander as the lawful incumbent at Canterbury. A number of English bishops refused to be consecrated by Stigand, choosing instead to go to Rome for the ceremony.

The year 1066 was one of three in English history that saw three kings on the throne. Edward the Confessor died in January; Harold Godwinson was crowned at Westminster in September; and William of Normandy successfully invaded England in October and took the crown from Harold, who lost his life at the Battle of Hastings. As archbishop, Stigand submitted to King William I (as he became) and attended his coronation on Christmas Day 1066. However, as he had no papal authority to carry out the coronation itself, the rite was probably performed by the Archbishop of York, Ealdred. Once the danger of rebellion against him was past, William had no further need of Stigand, and at the Council of Winchester in 1070 he was canonically deposed by the papal legate, Ermenfrid, and imprisoned at Winchester where he died in 1072 without regaining his liberty. He was, though, given an honourable burial in the minster.

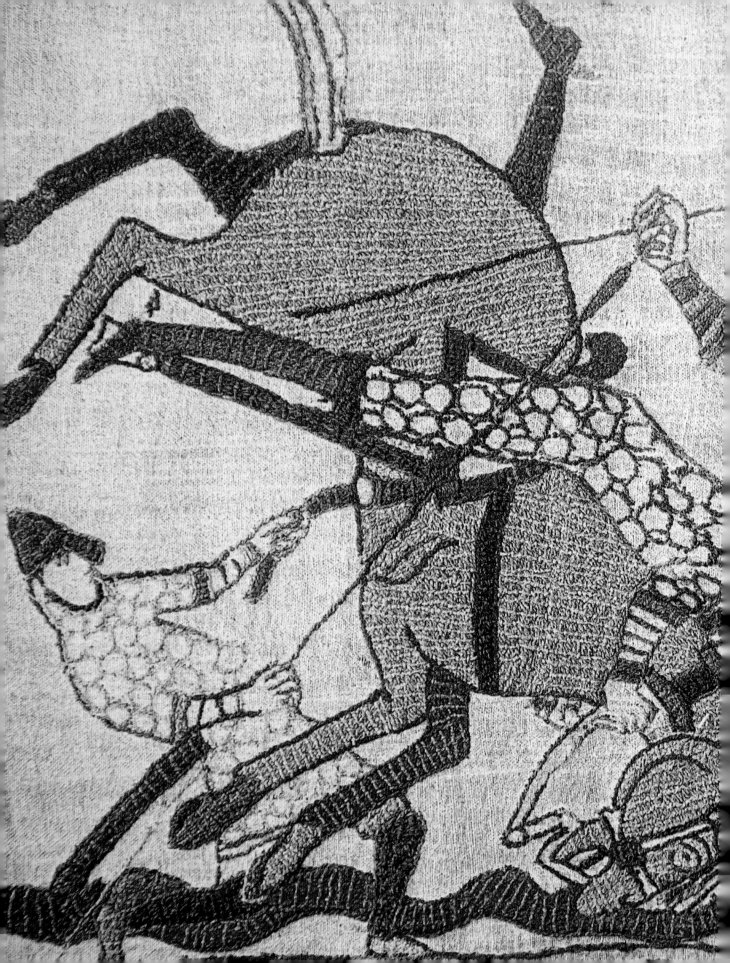

NORMAN AND ITALIAN INFLUENCES: 1070–1161

In 1067, a few months after the coronation of King William I, the ancient cathedral at Canterbury was largely destroyed by fire. The archbishop at the time was Stigand, who had managed to remain in office in spite of his appointment being declared unlawful by Pope Alexander II. However, when Stigand was canonically deposed at the Council of Winchester in 1070, William looked across the channel to Normandy for someone who could resurrect a new cathedral out of the ashes of the old. His choice fell upon Lanfranc, an Italian monk from Pavia who at the time was the Abbot of St Stephen's at Caen. Lanfranc was appointed archbishop in August 1070, a mere two weeks after Stigand's deposition, and although he was by then about sixty years of age, he set about his task with energy and enthusiasm.

Working closely with William, with whom he had co-operated to good effect before his conquest of England, Lanfranc embarked upon an extensive restructuring of the English Church. He vigorously asserted the supremacy of Canterbury over York; he tackled the continuing corruptions of simony and pluralism; and he gave Church synods new powers of management over their sees. And by preferring Normans to Englishmen when it came to senior ecclesiastical appointments, Lanfranc was steadily chipping away at the isolation of the English Church.

In all of this, Lanfranc's obedience to the King was more than simply a meeting of minds between two men who found the English temperament uncongenial: archbishops of Canterbury had by now become leading actors in the affairs of state, and William was entitled to expect Lanfranc's support. In return, he trusted his archbishop to act as vice-regent of England during his absences from the country – a trust that Lanfranc more than repaid when he foiled a conspiracy against the King that had been cooked up in 1075 by the Earls of Norfolk and Hereford. When William died in 1087, Lanfranc cleared the way for the crown to pass to his son William Rufus (King William II), further cementing his pivotal role in the imposition of Norman rule in England.

In Canterbury, Lanfranc set about rebuilding the fire-ravaged cathedral, and in only seven years (between 1070 and 1077) he had created a state-of-the-art Norman church with two western towers, a small choir that extended for only three bays to the east of the central crossing, and a squat tower topped by a golden seraph. He also reinvigorated the monastery, laying out a plan for the site that remained largely unchanged until its closure in 1540. Lanfranc's enthusiasm for building extended even to a palace for himself on a site to the north-west of the cathedral that is now occupied by a late 19th-century archbishop's palace.

When Lanfranc died of a fever in 1089, the archbishopric remained vacant for four years before being filled by another Italian, Anselm, who was born into a noble family in Lombardy and became Abbot of the Benedictine monastery of Bec, in Normandy. He was canonised as St Anselm in about 1170. Anselm's appointment to Canterbury was once again bound up with the complex interactions between Church and State. Following Lanfranc's death, the clergy wished

RIGHT: The building of Lanfranc's Norman cathedral, Canterbury Cathedral, Chapter House, 20th century

to see Anselm – who was already well known in England – appointed as his successor, but the king, William Rufus, refused to proceed. Only when he believed himself to be mortally ill at Christmas 1092 did William relent, summoning Anselm to hear his confession and administer the last rites. In fact, William was nowhere near death's door, and in March 1093 he finally appointed Anselm as archbishop. Anselm pleaded his unsuitability for the job, citing his age and poor health, but he finally relented and gave William the terms for his acceptance: the King had to return Church lands and property that he had seized; he had to accept the archbishop's spiritual counsel, and he had to acknowledge the authority of Pope Urban II over the English Church. William was loath to accept these conditions, consenting only to the first of them before quickly reneging even on that, but ecclesiastical and baronial pressure forced his hand. He returned the lands and revenues that he had appropriated, and in September 1093 Anselm was installed as archbishop.

The truce between King and Archbishop was, however, a fragile one, and Anselm's continuing opposition to royal interference in Church affairs led to his exile in 1097. While in Rome, he wrote one of the great works of early medieval theology – *Cur Deus Homo?* – in which he set out an explanation for the crucifixion of Jesus Christ (the satisfaction theory of atonement) that was to dominate Christian theology for centuries. Following the death of William Rufus in a hunting accident in the New Forest in 1100, the crown was seized in dramatic fashion by his brother, King Henry I, who invited Anselm to return from exile.

RIGHT: Lanfranc with the plans for his Norman cathedral, Canterbury Cathedral, Chapter House, 19th century

Anselm's opposition to the King's interference in Church matters continued and he was forced once again into exile in 1103; however, after exacting concessions from Henry, he returned to England in 1106 and spent the last three years of his life attending to the ecclesiastical affairs of Canterbury. He continued to press for the stricter observance of celibacy among the clergy and to defend the primacy of the province of Canterbury over York. Anselm's most enduring monument, however, was a major reconstruction of the cathedral that involved the demolition of the small crypt and choir at the eastern end of Lanfranc's church and their replacement with a new choir (also in the Norman style) that was unsurpassed in size and ornamentation. The choir itself was severely damaged by fire in 1174, but the crypt beneath, which was completed a little before 1100, is still in place.

Anselm died in 1109 and was succeeded as archbishop by his friend Ralph d'Escures, a French monk who had arrived in England in the previous year upon his appointment as Bishop of Rochester. D'Escures superintended the affairs of Canterbury for five years following Anselm's death until his own installation as archbishop in 1114. D'Escures did not, however, endear himself to Pope Pascal II, who felt that the English Church was pressing for too much autonomy. Like his immediate predecessors, d'Escures defended the primacy of Canterbury over York, and he refused to enthrone Thurstan of Bayeux as Archbishop of the northern province because of his refusal to acknowledge Canterbury's seniority. After d'Escures's death in 1122, Thurstan was finally confirmed at York by Pope Callixtus II.

Ralph d'Escures was succeeded by William de Corbeil, a Parisian who was appointed in July 1123. De Corbeil had previously been a secular canon at St Augustine's Abbey in Canterbury, and he was the first such canon to be elevated to the English episcopacy. Like his immediate predecessor, de Corbeil came into conflict with Thurstan of Bayeux, now installed as Archbishop of York, who not only refused to acknowledge de Corbeil's seniority over him but even visited the Pope to protest the validity of his election. There were, Thurstan claimed, a number of irregularities that could not be overlooked, including the fact that de Corbeil was not a monk. King Henry I persuaded Pope Callixtus II to set the objections aside, but following the Pope's death in 1124 the new Pope, Honorius II, pointedly refused to endorse the primacy of Canterbury. Two years later, Honorius made amends of a kind by appointing de Corbeil as papal legate in England and Scotland, thereby giving him canonical authority over Thurstan in York and, although Thurstan continued to pester the Pope on the matter, he failed to make much headway.

When William de Corbeil died in 1136 he was succeeded by Theobald, a Norman monk at the Benedictine abbey of Bec. King Henry I was now dead and Theobald's appointment in December 1138 was secured by King Stephen of England against the claims of Stephen's brother, Henry of Blois, the Bishop of Winchester. It was probably an appointment of political convenience, for Theobald had no significant connections in the Church apart from the reputation of his monastery at Bec (which had already supplied two archbishops of Canterbury, Lanfranc and Anselm).

Theobald's time as archbishop coincided with the turbulent civil war in England between King Stephen and his cousin, the Empress Matilda, who had a far more legitimate claim to the throne but was never able to muster enough support to usurp the King. Upon his election, Theobald swore fealty to Stephen, but the relationship between the two was a stormy one. When Stephen was imprisoned at Bristol in 1141 following the battle of Lincoln, Theobald sided with those who wished to see Matilda as queen, but once her campaign had patently failed, he returned to the King, helping to secure his release and ceremonially crowning him and his wife, Matilda of Boulogne, in 1141.

Theobald was at Stephen's deathbed in October 1154, and for the next six weeks he was regent of England until Stephen's chosen successor as king, Henry, Duke of Normandy, arrived in England. Theobald crowned him as King Henry II at Westminster in December 1154. This was one of Theobald's links with the terrible event that was soon to occur in Canterbury. The other was his commendation to Henry II of the promising young archdeacon of Canterbury, Thomas Becket. Thus it was that, when Theobald died in 1161, he had brought together the two men whose rivalry was to lead to one of the most infamous murders in world history.

RIGHT: King Stephen meets the Empress Matilda's army, led by the future Henry II, at Wallingford in 1153

MURDER IN THE CATHEDRAL AND DEATH IN THE HOLY LAND: 1162–1190

On 29 December 1170, an event occurred that shocked the whole of western medieval Christendom: Thomas Becket, Archbishop of Canterbury, was murdered in his own cathedral. The events leading up to the tragedy that was to make the name of Canterbury famous throughout the world are complex, but the outlines are straightforward enough. Becket was born in Cheapside in about 1120, the son of a wealthy London merchant. He was able, ambitious and well-educated and, in his twenties, he began to work in the household of the Archbishop of Canterbury, Theobald. Impressed with Becket's sharp mind and engaging personality, Theobald sent him to study canon law in Europe, and in 1154 he became Archdeacon of Canterbury. Becket's swift rise continued in the following year when, having been commended by Theobald to King Henry II, he was appointed Chancellor of England.

Though separated by a vast social chasm, the King and the Chancellor forged a strong personal relationship as well as a professional one. Indeed, Henry came to rely so much upon Becket's administrative and diplomatic skills that, when Theobald died in 1161, Henry turned to his Chancellor to fill the post. The King's motives in wishing to see Becket as Archbishop of Canterbury were largely self-interested. He had come to see the Church as a threat to some of his customary rights as King of England, and in Becket he believed he had a trusted ally with whom he could do business. He could not have been more wrong, for as soon as Becket became God's man, his loyalty lay with the Church. From the day of his enthronement in 1162, Becket made plain his determination to protect the privileges of the Church from the encroachments of the Crown, especially over the jurisdiction of ecclesiastical courts, and the two men who had once been almost as close as brothers became bitter adversaries.

Becket's eight years as Archbishop of Canterbury, most of which were spent in exile in France, were marked by increasingly angry confrontations between the two men as Becket refused to yield to Henry's demands for him to acknowledge the customary rights of the English Crown. Matters came to a head in December 1170 when Henry, celebrating Christmas with his court at Bur-le-Roi in Normandy, finally snapped. Furious at the continuation of Becket's defiance of his royal authority, Henry cursed the knights of his court as 'a nest of cowards and traitors who had allowed their lord to be treated with contempt by a low-born priest'. Hearing these words, four knights of the court slipped out, determined to please the King by silencing Becket. They rode to Canterbury and, in the late afternoon of 29 December, confronted the Archbishop inside the Cathedral. After a brief and furious exchange of words, the knights drew their swords and struck Becket violently about his body, killing him instantly and severing the crown of his head like the top of a boiled egg. Satisfied that the Archbishop would not rise again, they made their escape through the door into the cloisters by which they had entered.

RIGHT: St Thomas Becket, Canterbury Cathedral, Trinity Chapel, 20th century, using some medieval glass

Thomas Becket's murder in Canterbury Cathedral reverberated throughout Europe, and retribution was swift. Pope Alexander III declared Becket a martyr of the Church, and three years later, in 1173, he was canonised as St Thomas of Canterbury – an act that guaranteed Canterbury's status as one of Europe's leading centres of pilgrimage for the next three hundred and fifty years. The fate of the four knights is a matter of dispute: some historians believe that they returned to their ancestral lands in England, others that they were banished to the crusader kingdom of Jerusalem where they died fighting the infidel. As for King Henry, he performed an astonishing public act of penance: four years after the murder, in 1174, he walked barefoot through the streets of Canterbury to the cathedral where he prayed and fasted at Becket's tomb in the crypt after receiving physical chastisements from the monks.

Following Thomas Becket's death, the archbishopric remained vacant for almost four years. His eventual successor was Richard of Dover, but before his appointment in 1174, the job had first been offered to – and declined by – Roger, the Abbot of the Benedictine monastery of Bec. Much of Richard's time as archbishop, like that of his immediate predecessors, was spent arguing with the Archbishop of York (in Richard's case, Roger de Pont l'Evêque) over the respective status of the northern and southern provinces. He also clashed with the Abbot of St Augustine's Abbey over the monastery's claim of independence from the Archbishop. Richard was, however, far more co-operative with the King than Becket had been, leading many to believe that he was too weak in defending the liberties of the Church.

Richard of Dover died in 1184 and was succeeded by Baldwin, the son of an English clergyman who entered the Cistercian monastery at Forde, in Dorset, and later became Bishop of Worcester before his promotion to archbishop. Baldwin is especially remembered for his damaging confrontation with the monks of Canterbury. The problem sprang partly from the monks' resentment of the austerity and discipline that Baldwin tried to impose upon them and partly from their claim, which Baldwin disputed, to have a time-honoured role in the election of new archbishops. To escape their interference in matters that he regarded as beyond their remit, Baldwin set about establishing a college of secular canons at Hackington, a village just outside

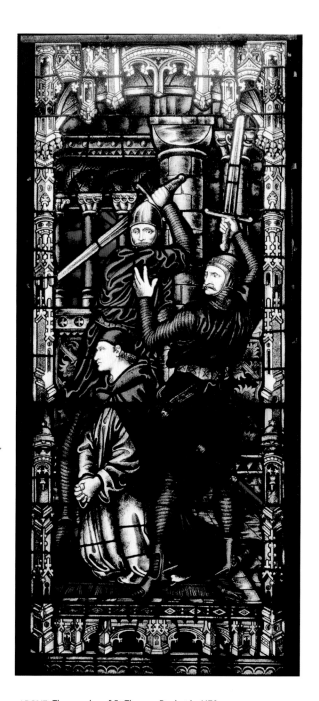

ABOVE: The murder of St Thomas Becket in 1170, Canterbury Cathedral, Chapter House, 20th century

Canterbury, which would enable him to exclude the monks from anything to do with the governance of the cathedral. This was seen by the monks as a deliberate provocation, and they struck back. At one time during the confrontation, they were virtually imprisoned in their own buildings for a year and a half. After dragging on for many years, the project at Hackington was finally abandoned through lack of papal support.

In 1188 Baldwin 'took the cross' and vowed to go on crusade to the Holy Land to recapture Jerusalem from the Islamic warrior Saladin. He had originally planned to go with Henry II, but the King died in July 1189 before the expedition could set off. Baldwin crowned Henry's successor, Richard I (the Lionheart), at Westminster and then accompanied the new King on the third crusade to the Holy Land in the following year. By now, however, Baldwin was in failing health and he died in November 1190 before the limited successes of the crusade had been won. The leadership of the English forces in the Holy Land was now taken over by the Bishop of Salisbury, Hubert Walter, a skilled administrator and diplomat who was largely responsible for raising the ransom for the King after the Lionheart had been captured near Vienna by the Duke of Austria on his way back to England. Hubert Walter's reward, in 1193, was to become Archbishop of Canterbury and Justiciar of England – in effect, the King's right-hand man.

LEFT: The penance of King Henry II in 1174, Canterbury Cathedral, Chapter House, 20th century

KING JOHN AND THE GREAT CHARTER: 1193–1228

Hubert Walter, who was installed as Archbishop of Canterbury in May 1193, is widely regarded as one of the most outstanding government ministers of medieval England. He began his career as a clerk to the exchequer and by the early 1180s had risen to the position of baron to the exchequer, in which capacity he rapidly became indispensable to King Henry II as a royal secretary. When Henry died in 1189, the new king, Richard I, appointed Walter to the bishopric of Salisbury and took him on the third crusade to the Holy Land. There he acted as Richard's spokesman in negotiating a peace treaty with the Islamic leader Saladin that gave Christians access to the Holy Sepulchre in Jerusalem. His promotion to Archbishop of Canterbury in 1193 gave him extensive powers to act on the King's behalf during Richard's lengthy absences from the country.

It was now that Walter's administrative abilities came to the fore as he found new ways of raising money for the king's army, set up a system of itinerant justices of the peace, and regulated the activities of Jewish moneylenders. He also created a system for keeping archival copies of all charters, patents and feet of fines. Following King Richard's death in 1199, Walter crowned his successor, King John, after helping him to beat off a challenge from his nephew, Arthur of Brittany. His reward this time was the Chancellorship of England, a position that enabled him to continue furthering the King's interests both at home and in France.

RIGHT: Carving on the tomb of Hubert Walter that may be a likeness of Saladin, Canterbury Cathedral, Trinity Chapel, 13th century

LEFT: The tomb of Hubert Walter, Canterbury Cathedral, Trinity Chapel, 13th century

ABOVE: The sealing of Magna Carta by King John at Runnymede in 1215, 19th century illustration by John Leech

Hubert Walter has never been regarded as either a particularly holy or learned archbishop, and he was frequently at odds with the monks of Canterbury; but he left an enduring mark on the administration of the country. He died in July 1205 and was buried in the newly completed Trinity Chapel at Canterbury where his tomb still stands. It is the oldest tomb in the cathedral, and one of the beautifully carved heads that encircles the sarcophagus is thought to be that of his erstwhile adversary, Saladin. The wooden crescent affixed to a nearby vault may also be one of his trophies from the crusades.

After Walter's death, the cathedral community was thrown into confusion over the succession. The monks of the cathedral elected Reginald, their sub-prior, but King John ignored their wishes and instead chose the Bishop of Norwich, John de Grey. Both names, however, were rejected by Pope Innocent III who ordered the monks to elect Stephen Langton, an English cardinal who was widely regarded as the leading churchman of his day. This they did, and Langton was duly installed as archbishop in June 1207. There then ensued a bitter political struggle between King and Pope, with Langton at the eye of the storm. King John railed against those who had supported Langton, and he sent the monks into exile in Flanders. In the following year (1208) Pope Innocent hit back by placing England under an interdict – an ecclesiastical censure prohibiting the celebration of most of the sacraments. In 1212, after the failure of repeated negotiations, Innocent took the dramatic step of passing a sentence of deposition against John. It was the decisive blow. John finally yielded and England became a fiefdom of the Holy See. Langton returned from exile in France and absolved the King, who swore to repeal the unjust laws he had enacted and to restore the customary liberties of the Church. Almost immediately he violated his oath.

In the turmoil that followed, Langton became a leader in the struggle against the King. In concert with the barons, he finally forced John to put his seal on a seminal document – Magna Carta – that the Archbishop himself had helped to draft. Sealed at Runnymede on 15 June 1215, it protected the freedoms of the Church, outlawed the arbitrary arrest and imprisonment of citizens, and placed limitations on feudal payments to the crown. In the short term, however, Magna Carta was a flop. Since John now held his kingdom as a fiefdom of the Holy See, the Pope was obliged to defend his interests, and he ordered Langton to excommunicate those who had forced John to the table at Runnymede. Langton refused and was suspended from all his archiepiscopal functions. When he appealed against the order, the Pope changed his mind and lifted the suspension on the condition that Langton once again left England. But in 1216 both King John and Pope Innocent III died, and two years later the Archbishop was able once again to return from exile. On 7 July 1220, in one of the great religious festivals of early medieval Europe, he presided over the transfer of St Thomas Becket's relics from their tomb in the crypt of the cathedral to the magnificent gilded shrine that had been constructed in the Trinity Chapel above. Known as the festival of the translation of the relics, it assured Canterbury's destiny as one of the great pilgrimage centres of Europe.

Stephen Langton died in 1228 and was buried in the apse of what was then the Norman chapel of St Michael in the south-west transept of the cathedral. When the chapel was rebuilt in the gothic style in the 15th century to accommodate the sumptuous tomb of Lady Margaret Holland and her two husbands, Langton's relatively modest tomb was displaced, so the eastern wall of the chapel was altered to straddle the coffin. He is still there, with his body inside the cathedral and his feet outside – a somewhat undignified resting place for a great scholar, an indefatigable negotiator and a wise elder statesman.

IN THE SHADOW
OF GREATNESS: 1229–1313

After a glittering array of luminaries (Alphege, Lanfranc, Anselm, Theobald, Becket, Walter and Langton), the roll-call of archbishops who followed Stephen Langton contained a number of lesser lights. After Langton's death in 1228, the monks of the cathedral elected one of their own, Walter d'Eynsham, to be the next archbishop. There must, however, have been some doubts about his suitability, for he was subjected to a theological examination by a group of cardinals and was found wanting. As a result, Pope Gregory IX refused to allow the appointment. King Henry III then turned to Richard le Grant, a distinguished scholar who at the time was Chancellor of Lincoln Cathedral. With the support of the Pope and the English bishops, le Grant was installed as Archbishop of Canterbury in June 1229.

Once in office, le Grant clashed with the King over his demands for the payment of a scutage of three marks (a tax levied on baronial tenants of the crown), and he also came into conflict with the Chief Justiciar of England, Hubert de Burgh, over the territorial rights of the see of Canterbury. An enthusiastic reformer, le Grant (like several of his predecessors) attacked the system of pluralism that allowed priests to hold multiple benefices and pay others to carry out the duties attached to them. He even travelled to Rome to enlist the help of the Vatican in his endeavours. He was favourably received, but he died in Italy in the summer of 1231 on his way home and was buried in the Umbrian town of San Gemini.

The events that followed Richard le Grant's death were now beginning to follow a familiar pattern. The monks of the cathedral first elected Ralph Neville, the Chancellor of England, to be their new archbishop, but the election was set aside by Pope Gregory IX on the grounds of Neville's lack of learning. The monks then elected their prior, John of Sittingbourne, but his election was also quashed by a papal court in 1232. The third choice of the monks was John Blund, a noted English philosopher who taught at Oxford University, but he too was rejected by the Pope.

Eventually the name of Edmund Rich emerged as an acceptable candidate to all the parties with an interest in the election, and he was installed as archbishop in April 1234. Rich was a pious man whose life was one of self-denial and charity towards others. He fasted regularly, wore a hair shirt and spent much of each night in prayer and meditation. A lecturer in mathematics and dialectics at Oxford University, he was said often to be so tired from his nightly devotions that he dropped off to sleep in his own lectures. Though a man of gentle disposition, Rich soon came into conflict with King Henry III, threatening him with excommunication if he continued to ride roughshod over the counsels of the barons and bishops. He also clashed with the Canterbury monks, excommunicating a number of them in 1239, and he even had to resort to litigation to exercise his archiepiscopal rights of visitation to the monasteries.

Edmund Rich died near Pontigny, in Burgundy, in November 1240 while on his way to Rome. His body was never repatriated, possibly because the monks resented what they regarded as his

RIGHT: St Edmund Rich, Canterbury Cathedral, Chapter House, 19th century

Saint Edmund

attacks on their independence and didn't want him back. He was buried in the Cistercian abbey church at Pontigny where his relics now rest in a baroque 17th-century casket. He was canonised as St Edmund Rich in 1246, the last Archbishop of Canterbury to be made a saint. He was succeeded by Boniface of Savoy, a Frenchman of noble descent who was consecrated archbishop in 1241. The English chronicler Matthew Paris said of him that he was noted more for his birth than his brains, and this, combined with an overbearing manner and his frequent absences in France, made Boniface unpopular with the English bishops. He was, however, vigorous in defending the interests of his see, and he successfully freed it from the crippling debt (of some 22,000 marks) that he had inherited. The early English gothic chapel at Lambeth Palace dates from work carried out in Boniface's time. It still stands.

After Boniface's death in 1270, the monks elected their prior, Adam de Chillenden, as their new archbishop, but once again the election was set aside by Rome. To end the dispute, Pope Gregory X appointed Robert Kilwardby, a member of the Dominican Order of Preachers and a teacher of grammar and logic at Oxford University. He was installed as Archbishop of Canterbury in February 1273, and in the following year he crowned King Edward I (Edward Longshanks) and Queen Eleanor of Castile. This apart, Kilwardby took little interest in the political affairs of England. In 1278 he was appointed by Pope Nicholas III as Cardinal Bishop of Porto-Santa Rufina in Italy and he left Canterbury, taking with him important papers, registers and documents belonging to the see. At his departure, Canterbury was once again deep in debt, for Kilwardby had managed to undo the financial order achieved by his predecessor, Boniface. He died in 1279 and was buried in the Dominican convent at Viterbo, in Italy.

Robert Kilwardby's death allowed Edward Longshanks to appoint his close ally Robert Burnell, the Bishop of what was now the united diocese of Bath and Wells, to be the new Archbishop of Canterbury, but his election in the summer of 1278 was quashed by Pope Nicholas III. The King sent a delegation to Rome to try to change the Pope's mind, but Burnell was once again passed over in favour of one of the delegates, the pious and principled Franciscan friar, John Peckham (or Pecham). He became archbishop in February 1279.

A prickly but learned man, Peckham had debated with Thomas Aquinas when they were together in Paris in about 1270. He was influenced in his thinking by the English scientist, Roger Bacon, whom he must also have met when they were both at the same Franciscan friary in France. Peckham's period in office was noted for his insistence on priestly discipline and his contention that Jews should either convert to Christianity or face persecution. He played a lesser role than some of his predecessors in the political issues of his day, though – in an echo of Becket's earlier conflict with Henry II – he clashed with King Edward I over the respective jurisdictions of royal and ecclesiastical courts. Being a friar, he had no personal property or income to help with the expenses of his office, and he left the see of Canterbury in considerable debt. After his death in December 1292, Peckham's body was buried in the Martyrdom at Canterbury where his tomb still survives, but his heart was interred beneath the high altar of the church of St Francis of Assisi in Notting Hill, London.

John Peckham was succeeded by Robert Winchelsey, a theologian in the medieval scholastic tradition. Upright, stern and determined, he was more feared than liked, and his life was one of penance, chastity and religious devotion. Although he initially had the support of King Edward I,

Winchelsey later became a forceful opponent, particularly over Edward's attempts to tax the clergy in order to further his military campaigns in France. Backed by Pope Boniface VIII, the Archbishop encouraged his clergy to refuse any further royal demands for tax. Edward retaliated by condemning the rebellious clerics as traitors and ordering their property to be seized. Resistance among them eventually crumbled and most of the clergy paid up, but Winchelsey himself refused and the King simply grabbed many of his lands and manors.

Further demands for reform by Winchelsey fuelled Edward's belief that the Archbishop was plotting against him and, at the King's instigation, he was suspended by Pope Clement V. In 1306 he went into exile in France where he stayed until Edward's death in the following year. The new king – Longshank's son Edward II – petitioned the Pope for Winchelsey's restoration; it was a fatal miscalculation, for on his return to England in 1308, the Archbishop allied himself with those who were opposed to Edward's increasingly embarrassing association with Piers Gaveston and his favouritism towards the Despenser family. Four years later, in 1312, Winchelsey passed a suspended sentence of excommunication on Gaveston – though it was later lifted by his successor, Walter Reynolds. After Robert Winchelsey's death in 1313, a modest cult grew up around him and miracles were alleged to have occurred at his tomb in Canterbury, but attempts to have him canonised proved unsuccessful.

THE WARRING PLANTAGENETS: 1313–1348

After Robert Winchelsey's death in 1313, the monks of the cathedral tried and failed to have their candidate accepted by the Pope. This time their misplaced choice fell upon Thomas Cobham, a noted theologian who later became Bishop of Worcester. After Cobham's rejection, King Edward II successfully petitioned Pope Clement V to appoint the current Bishop of Worcester, Walter Reynolds, as the next Archbishop of Canterbury, and he was duly installed in January 1314.

Reynolds, the son of a baker of Windsor, began his ecclesiastical career as a chaplain in the service of King Edward I (Edward Longshanks) where his somewhat theatrical mannerisms appealed to the King's young son, who succeeded his father onto the throne in 1307 as King Edward II. By this time, Reynolds was Bishop of Worcester, but he seems to have been a poor counsellor for the new King, failing to warn him of growing public unease over his obsessions and generally abetting him in his pleasures and follies. Eventually, however, dissatisfaction with Edward's conduct reached the point where Reynolds, now Archbishop of Canterbury, could no longer remain silent. He summonsed the bishops to St Paul's in December 1321 and told them that the English realm, which had 'once rejoiced in the beauty of peace', was now in danger of 'shipwreck through civil war'.

It was a turning point in Edward II's increasingly chaotic reign. In 1325 his wife Isabella, who had been sent to France to negotiate a peace treaty, turned against her husband and took the exiled Roger Mortimer, a powerful warlord from the Marches, as her lover. In the following year, Isabella and Mortimer invaded England with a small army and Edward fled. Early in 1327, he was forced to abdicate in favour of his fourteen-year-old son, who was crowned by Reynolds as King Edward III. Before the year was out, Reynolds had died at Mortlake and the deposed Edward II – now plain Edward of Caernarfon – had died at Berkeley Castle in Gloucestershire, probably at the hand of an assassin.

Following Walter Reynolds's death, a tussle broke out between Isabella and Mortimer on the one hand and Henry, Earl of Lancaster on the other over his successor as archbishop. Lancaster prevailed and Simon Meopham was appointed in December 1327, but he was not a great success. According to a local chronicler, William Thorne, he was considered to be a man of 'no great ability and with scant knowledge of ecclesiastical tradition and propriety'. His attempted visitations to the see of Canterbury were keenly resented by some of the secular clergy, and his rulings over the benefices of certain Kentish churches were vigorously disputed by the monks of St Augustine's who appealed to the papal nuncio, Icherius de Concareto. Meopham's refusal to cooperate with the investigation led to his excommunication in 1333 by Pope John XXII.

Concareto's adjudication eventually found against the Archbishop and he was ordered to pay the monks £700 in costs, but he died before the order could be enforced. After Meopham's death, the excommunication was lifted allowing him to be buried at Canterbury where his black marble tomb still stands at the entrance to St Anselm's Chapel.

Simon Meopham's successor, John de Stratford, was born in Stratford-upon-Avon and educated at Oxford. He served in the household of Archbishop Robert Winchelsey and he went on to accumulate a large portfolio of benefices before being appointed Bishop of Winchester by Pope John XXII in 1323. While there, de Stratford sided with Queen Isabella in her struggle against her husband, Edward II, visiting the captive King at Kenilworth and urging him to abdicate in favour of his son. Upon Edward III's accession to the throne in 1327, de Stratford became a leading member of the King's council, and following Roger Mortimer's downfall and execution in 1330, he was appointed Chancellor of England.

De Stratford's power base, already formidable, was further strengthened with his appointment as Archbishop of Canterbury in 1333, and he was effectively regent of England during Edward's increasingly costly forays on the continent. But the two eventually fell out – spectacularly – when the King returned from a sortie to Flanders in December 1340 humiliated, impecunious and angry. Desperately searching for a scapegoat, he turned on de Stratford, publicly accusing him of obstructing the collection of taxes and generally abusing his authority. The Archbishop was unmoved, replying to Edward's tirade with equally angry words and accusing him of traducing both Magna Carta and his coronation oath. De Stratford was now in deep waters, on the cusp of a charge of treason and all too aware of the fate that had befallen his predecessor, Thomas Becket, in not dissimilar circumstances. The crisis peaked in 1341 when de Stratford was brought before a rigged court at the palace of Westminster to face thirty-two charges of misconduct. But the whole weight of public support lay behind the Archbishop, and what could have become a disaster for him was averted when Edward was forced, humiliatingly, to climb down.

Archbishop and King were eventually reconciled, but by now the high watermark of de Stratford's career was over. He died at his manor of Mayfield, in Sussex, in August 1348 and was buried at Canterbury where his tomb, damaged by the ravages of time, still stands in the south choir aisle. Edward III had almost another thirty years on the throne.

RIGHT: The deposition of King Edward II at Kenilworth Castle in 1327

THE PLAGUE, THE POLL TAX AND RELIGIOUS RADICALISM: 1349–1396

John de Stratford was succeeded initially by the Dean of Lincoln, John de Ufford, but his appointment by King Edward III was challenged – unsuccessfully – by the Canterbury monks whose preferred candidate was Thomas Bradwardine, a trusted confessor of the King, whom he had attended at the battle of Crécy in 1346. De Ufford's election was confirmed by Pope Clement VI in September 1348, but he succumbed to the Black Death before he could take up the office. His name appears in some listings of the archbishops of Canterbury but not others. De Ufford's place was then taken by Bradwardine, the monks' original candidate, who became archbishop in July 1349; he too died of the plague a mere forty days later.

The Black Death also dominated the archiepiscopate of Bradwardine's successor, Simon Islip, who was appointed in December 1349. Although he himself managed to evade the disease, Islip had to deal with the ravages it inflicted on the many parishes that were losing priests as well as parishioners. Those who survived were tempted to take advantage of their scarcity value by increasing the fees they charged for their services. Islip tried to halt the abuse – in the process earning a reputation for meanness. His attempts to sharpen the professionalism of the clergy were, however, well meant, and in his will, he left money to endow a new college – Canterbury College – at Oxford. Intended for the education of both monks and secular clergy, it flourished for almost two hundred years before being absorbed into Christ Church by Cardinal Wolsey in the 1520s; but its erstwhile site is still marked by the Canterbury Quadrangle near the current college library.

Simon Islip died in April 1366 and was buried at Canterbury, though his tomb no longer survives. His successor was intended to be William Edington, the Bishop of Winchester, but he declined the office for reasons of ill health. Instead, Simon Langham – the Bishop of Ely and Chancellor of England – was promoted to archbishop in July 1366. Two years later, Langham was appointed by Pope Urban V as cardinal priest of San Sisto Vecchio in Rome, a move that displeased the King as Langham had failed to consult him before taking the cardinal's cap. Edward retaliated by seizing some of Canterbury's revenues, prompting Langham to resign as archbishop and take himself to the papal court at Avignon. He was re-elected archbishop for a second time by the monks of Canterbury in 1374 following the death of Archbishop William Whittlesey, but he withdrew his candidature when neither the King nor the Pope supported him. When the papacy moved back to Rome in 1376, Langham was given permission to return to England where he still held several benefices, but he died at Avignon before setting out. His body was repatriated for burial in Westminster Abbey.

Simon Langham was succeeded by William Whittlesey, who was a canon at Lichfield, Chichester and Lincoln before being appointed to bishoprics at Rochester and Worcester. He was promoted to Canterbury in October 1368, but owing to his feeble health and preference

for solitude, his term of office was uneventful. Whittlesey died at Lambeth in June 1374 and was succeeded by an altogether more substantial figure, Simon Sudbury. As Bishop of London, Sudbury had made himself very useful to Edward III in various diplomatic missions to Calais and Flanders, and his reward was promotion to Canterbury. He became archbishop in 1375 and conducted Edward's funeral in June 1377 before crowning the young Richard II (the son of the Black Prince and grandson of Edward III) later that year. In 1378 Sudbury presided over the interrogation at Lambeth of the proto-reformer John Wycliffe, whose stinging attacks on the wealth of the Church and the privileges of the clergy were an embarrassment to those in high places. A case was prepared for consideration by Pope Gregory XI, but Gregory died before it could be heard and Wycliffe was free to continue his outspoken attacks on Roman doctrine and practice.

In 1380 Sudbury was appointed Chancellor of England, a position that thrust him into a leading role in imposing the widely reviled poll tax. It was the spark that lit the Peasants' Revolt. In June 1381 Kentish insurgents led by Wat Tyler marched on London and, with the connivance of the guards, they stormed the Tower where Sudbury was hiding. While the King, Richard II, was meeting a deputation of rebels at Mile End, Sudbury was dragged by the mob to Tower Hill and beheaded – the third Archbishop of Canterbury (after Alphege and Becket) to meet a violent death. His body was returned to Canterbury where his large and austere tomb still stands in the cathedral, but his head, which had been impaled on London Bridge, was taken to St Gregory's church in his native Suffolk town of Sudbury. There is a persistent story that his tomb at Canterbury contains a cannonball instead of a head. Sudbury's legacy to Canterbury is the glorious perpendicular gothic nave constructed by Henry Yvele, the most accomplished master-builder of his day. Sudbury personally contributed at least £2,000 towards the cost, and he also paid for the reconstruction of Canterbury's west gate.

Simon Sudbury was succeeded by William Courtenay, the son of the tenth Earl of Devon and a great-grandson of King Edward I. He came to Canterbury from the bishopric of London at a time when the radical theological beliefs of John Wycliffe and his followers were gaining momentum. The year after his appointment, in 1382, Courtenay summoned a synod at Blackfriars. Popularly known as the 'Earthquake Synod' because of the tremor that shook the City of London while it was meeting, it condemned many of Wycliffe's views, particularly his affirmation of the doctrine of predestination and his dismissal of monks and friars as 'the pests of society, the enemies of religion, and

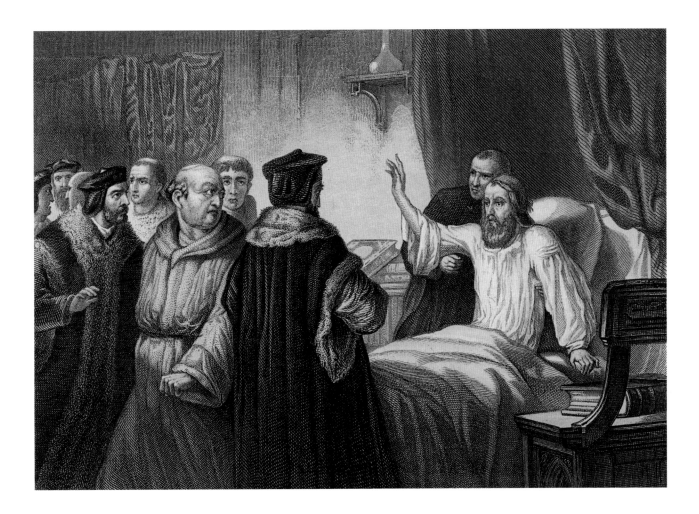

ABOVE: John Wycliffe
assailed by the Friars on his
sickbed at Oxford in 1378

LEFT: Simon of Sudbury,
Canterbury Cathedral,
Chapter House, 19th century

the promoters of every crime'. Courtenay subsequently took a personal interest in seeking out Wycliffe's supporters, commonly known as Lollards.

William Courtenay was appointed Chancellor of England in 1381 and in the following year he conducted the marriage of King Richard II to Anne of Bohemia. Later, however, he publicly upbraided the King for his extravagant lifestyle and his questionable choice of courtiers and, after an angry scene in which the King actually drew his sword against the Archbishop and threatened to run him through, he fled for a time to his native Devon disguised as a monk. Courtenay died at Maidstone in 1396 and was buried at Canterbury next to the tomb of the Black Prince in the Trinity Chapel.

RED AND WHITE ROSES: 1396–1486

Like his predecessor William Courtenay, Thomas Arundel was born into the nobility: his father was the tenth Earl of Arundel and his mother was from the powerful house of Lancaster. With such privileged connections, Arundel rose quickly through the ecclesiastical ranks, becoming Archbishop of York in 1388 and of Canterbury in 1396. He served twice as Chancellor of England during the reign of Richard II, and he conducted Richard's second marriage to Isabella, the daughter of Charles VI of France. By 1397 Arundel's position appeared unassailable. But life under the fickle King was rarely straightforward and Richard, having assured his archbishop of his confidence in him, banished him for the part he had played in setting up a commission of regency to govern the country during the early years of his reign. When Arundel went to Rome to plead his case with Pope Boniface IX, the King took the opportunity provided by his absence to appoint Roger Walden, the Dean of York, in his place.

Walden's time as archbishop was short and largely inconsequential, for the exiled Arundel joined another outcast, Henry Bolingbroke, in a plot to return to England, seize the crown from Richard II, and proclaim Bolingbroke (the son of John of Gaunt and grandson of Edward III) as king. The plan worked: when Bolingbroke returned, large numbers of fighting men flocked to his banner and Richard formally surrendered the crown at Flint Castle in September 1399. Thomas Arundel was restored to Canterbury, and the unfortunate Roger Walden was demoted to the

RIGHT: The tomb of King Henry IV and Queen Joan of Navarre, Canterbury Cathedral, Trinity Chapel, 15th century

LEFT: The tomb of Henry Chichele, Canterbury Cathedral, Choir, 15th century

Lancaster Rose　　　*York Rose*　　　*Tudor Rose*

bishopric of London. Following Bolingbroke's coronation as King Henry IV, Arundel served him twice as Chancellor of England, but his relationship with the Crown deteriorated when Henry died in 1413 and was succeeded by his son, King Henry V. Arundel's face no longer fitted, and when he suffered a stroke that left him speechless in 1414, the King secured the appointment of Henry Chichele in his place.

Chichele came from humble origins in Northamptonshire. He was educated at Winchester and Oxford and became an advocate in the principal ecclesiastical court, the Court of Arches. In 1405 he began his diplomatic career by visiting Pope Innocent VII, where he may have played a part in finally ending the schism in the papacy between Rome and the remaining anti-popes in Avignon. Whatever Chichele's exact role, he and his fellow emissaries were held in high esteem – not least by Henry V, who in 1414 recommended him to Pope Gregory XII as the successor to Thomas Arundel.

As archbishop, Chichele placed his legal and diplomatic skills at the service of the King. He negotiated the terms for the surrender of Rouen in 1419 and he arranged the legalities of Henry V's marriage to Catherine of Valois. In 1421 he crowned her queen of England and baptised her child, later to become Henry VI. Chichele was, like his immediate predecessors, an ardent persecutor of heretics, hunting down and excommunicating Lollards and other supporters of John Wycliffe. He was also assiduous in defending the privileges of the see of Canterbury, negotiating with the King's ministers to minimise the amount of tax that was levied on clerical endowments. In 1438 Chichele personally contributed to the foundation of All Souls College at Oxford.

Henry Chichele died in 1443 and was buried at Canterbury in a spectacular tomb that has effigies of him both as Archbishop in full regalia and as a near-naked corpse on the day of judgement. Erected by the fellows of All Souls College, it is a stark reminder that however great and glorious an archbishop's earthly achievements may be, he stands equally before God with the rest of humanity on the day of judgement. The inscription round the tomb reads: 'I was pauper-born, then to primate raised. Now I am cut down and served up for worms. Behold my grave.'

RIGHT: King Henry V

Before he died, Chichele nominated his successor, John Stafford, for reasons of his 'high intellectual and moral qualifications, the nobility of his birth, the influence of his relations, and his almost boundless hospitality'. In fact, Stafford was the illegitimate son of a Wiltshire squire,

Edwardus princeps Wallie &
primus filius Edwardi quarti

Ricardus dux Eboraci secundus
filius Edwardi quarti

Sir Humphrey Stafford; in spite of his bastardy, he was allowed to study law at Oxford and became Lord Privy Seal in 1421, Lord Treasurer in 1422 and Lord Chancellor of England in 1432. He was appointed Archbishop of Canterbury in September 1443, a position that he held until his death in 1452.

Stafford's administrative experience and political acumen made him a valuable counsellor to the inept King Henry VI. He played an influential part in negotiating Henry's marriage to Margaret of Anjou and he officiated at their wedding in April 1445. Little else of note has been recorded of Stafford's activities as archbishop, though it is known that in August 1451 he received the King on a pilgrimage to the shrine of Thomas Becket. It was probably his last public appearance.

John Stafford died at Maidstone in 1452 and was buried in the Martyrdom at Canterbury. He was succeeded in the same year by Cardinal John Kemp, who had already had a long and successful career both in the Church, where he was Cardinal Archbishop of York, and as an international diplomat in the service of Henry V. He served twice as Lord Chancellor of England and was described by Henry VI as 'one of the wisest lords of the land'. But towards the end of his life, when former Plantagenet lands in France were being lost and Henry was on a rapidly downward mental path, Kemp's popularity waned and he became known as 'the curséd cardinal' who had allowed his see to fall into a state of some disorder. He died suddenly at Lambeth in 1454, having served less than two years as Archbishop, and was buried in the choir at Canterbury where his tomb still stands.

John Kemp's successor, Cardinal Thomas Bourgchier, was a younger son of Sir William Bourgchier who had fought with King Henry V at the Battle of Agincourt in 1415. His mother, Anne of Gloucester, was a granddaughter of Edward III. Bourgchier was appointed Archbishop of Canterbury in April 1454 at a time when the Wars of the Roses were about to erupt between the houses of Lancaster and York. At first, Bourgchier maintained a non-partisan position in the dynastic struggle, acting as a mediator between the two factions, but in 1459 he sided with the Yorkists, crowning the young Edward IV as the first Yorkist King of England in 1461. Four years later he crowned Edward's ambitious and politically astute wife, Elizabeth Woodville, as queen consort.

Following the sudden death of Edward IV in April 1483, Bourgchier persuaded the widowed queen to allow her younger son, Richard, to join his older brother Edward, Prince of Wales, in the Tower of London. Neither was to emerge from it alive. They are presumed to have been murdered, though their bodies have never been unambiguously identified and their probable assassin is still disputed. Although Bourgchier himself was not implicated in the murders – and was presumably appalled by them – he was obliged to officiate at the coronation of King Richard III, the last of the Plantagenet kings, in July 1483. He did, though, absent himself from the coronation banquet. Following Richard's defeat at the Battle of Bosworth Field in 1485, Bourgchier crowned the victor, Henry Tudor, as King Henry VII and later conducted his marriage to Princess Elizabeth of York, the eldest daughter of Edward IV and Elizabeth Woodville. Thus at a stroke, the Wars of the Roses had ended and the Tudor dynasty had begun. Two months after Henry and Elizabeth's wedding, in March 1486, Thomas Bourgchier died at his palatial residence of Knole, near Sevenoaks, after holding office as archbishop for thirty-two years. He was buried in the choir at Canterbury where his large and ornate tomb still stands.

LEFT: Richard, Duke of York and Edward, Prince of Wales (the princes in the Tower), Canterbury Cathedral, northwest transept, 15th century

THE ROAD TO REFORMATION: 1486–1532

The career of Cardinal John Morton, who succeeded Thomas Bourgchier as Archbishop of Canterbury in October 1486, first blossomed during the Wars of the Roses when he threw in his lot with the house of Lancaster. Once the Battle of Tewksbury in May 1471 had ended Lancastrian ambitions, however, Morton transferred his allegiance to the Yorkist Edward IV and was used by him in various diplomatic missions in Europe. He was ambassador to the French court of Louis XI in 1477, and after Edward's death in 1483, he assisted in the execution of his will. But with the accession of Richard III, Morton, who by now had been consecrated Bishop of Ely, joined the opposition to the new king. He was arrested and handed over to the custody of the Duke of Buckingham at Brecknock Castle, from where he escaped to Flanders and joined the exiled Henry Tudor in his designs upon the English throne. Following Henry's accession to the throne in 1485 as King Henry VII, Morton was appointed Archbishop of Canterbury. In the following year, he became Lord Chancellor and in 1493 he was created a cardinal.

As Chancellor, Morton had the task of restoring the depleted coffers of the Tudor king, and he did so through the use of a creative tax-gathering device that has come to be known as Morton's Fork. Morton explained it to those whose job it was to relieve the citizenry of their money: 'If the subject is seen to live frugally, tell him because he is clearly a money saver of great ability, he can afford to give generously to the king. If, however, the subject lives a life of great extravagance, tell him he, too, can afford to give largely, the proof of his opulence being evident in his expenditure.' Thus everybody, rich and poor alike, had to stump up. It was an early version of 'catch–22'.

Morton was a fierce but incorruptible defender of Canterbury's interests and one of the great builders of the age. He was responsible for the Old Palace at Hatfield House – where Queen Elizabeth I spent much of her childhood – and he built the familiar redbrick Tudor gatehouse at Lambeth Palace that is still known as Morton's Tower. It was at Lambeth that Morton acted as mentor to the young Thomas More when he was a page in the Archbishop's household. At Canterbury, Morton built and largely financed the crowning glory of the present cathedral – the supremely elegant central tower, known as Bell Harry, which ranks as one of the finest achievements of high gothic art.

John Morton died at his palace of Knole, near Sevenoaks, in September 1500 and was buried in the crypt at Canterbury. His nearby cenotaph was once an elaborate and colourful structure but has since suffered from neglect as well as the destructive iconoclasm of the 17th-century Puritans. It is, though, still possible to enjoy the visual puns on his name that adorn the edifice. The task of following in such illustrious footsteps fell initially to Thomas Langton, the popular Bishop of Winchester who was elected in January 1501, but he died of the plague only five days later. He was never enthroned and is not normally included in the list of archbishops.

RIGHT: The gatehouse (Morton's Tower), Lambeth Palace, London

Langton was succeeded in the same year by Henry Deane who, having earlier served as prior of the Augustinian house at Llanthony in Monmouthshire, was the first monk to be appointed archbishop since Simon Langham in 1366. He was also the last.

Deane's occupancy of the office was short and the records of his primacy are sparse. He negotiated the Treaty of Perpetual Peace between England and Scotland in 1502, and he arranged the marriage of Henry VII's daughter, Margaret Tudor, to James IV of Scotland. He also officiated at the marriage of Arthur, Prince of Wales, to Catherine of Aragon in November 1501 – but that was about it. Deane died in February 1503, and after an elaborately theatrical funeral procession from Lambeth to Canterbury, he was buried in the Martyrdom in the north-west transept, close to the site of Thomas Becket's murder. He was succeeded by William Warham, the last Archbishop of Canterbury before the tectonic shifts of the Reformation that were fundamentally to change the religious life of England.

Warham was educated at Winchester and Oxford before embarking upon a legal career that saw him become principal of the Civil Law School at Oxford and (in 1494) Master of the Rolls. He later took holy orders. Warham was favoured by King Henry VII as a clever diplomat, and it was he who arranged the marriage between the Prince of Wales and Catherine of Aragon. Further appointments followed swiftly: Bishop of London and Keeper of the Great Seal in 1502, Archbishop of Canterbury in 1503, and Lord Chancellor in 1504. Following the death of Henry VII in 1509, Warham crowned his successor, King Henry VIII.

Warham never fully gained the new King's confidence, and in 1515 he resigned as Lord Chancellor. He was succeeded in the office by Thomas Wolsey, whom he had earlier consecrated Cardinal Archbishop of York – a position that technically outranked his own. Thereafter, however, Warham seems often to have played second fiddle to the much younger and far more ambitious Wolsey. It was Wolsey who organised the grandiose meeting between Henry VIII and Francis I of France in 1520 – the Field of the Cloth of Gold – and it was Wolsey who led the secret enquiry into the validity of the royal marriage in 1527. Once the divorce proceedings between Henry and Catherine were under way, Warham was appointed counsel to the Queen, but he was now a frail and elderly man unable effectively to oppose the King's wishes, and he meekly signed the letter to Pope Clement VII urging him to annul the marriage.

It was much the same story with the Convocation of Canterbury, presided over by Warham in 1531–32. It was convened to ratify Henry's demand for the Church to renounce its authority to make ecclesiastical laws without royal consent. Warham tried to prevaricate, but the King would have none of it. Accompanied by his councillors in parliament, Henry made a speech in May 1532 accusing the clergy of still being half-loyal to Rome. It was a humiliation for Warham, and later that month the Convocation accepted what has come to be known as the Submission of the Clergy. The best that Warham could do was to secure the insertion of the face-saving clause: '… so far as the law of Christ allows'. The settlement was confirmed in 1534, after Warham's death,

when the Reformation Parliament passed the Act for the Submission of the Clergy and the Restraint of Appeals.

In his later years, Warham was more at home in his role as Chancellor of Oxford University at a time when the revival of English scholarship was revitalising the intellectual life of the nation. He delighted in the company of scholars and was liberal in his support of the literary enterprises undertaken by the university. He also became a staunch supporter of the Dutch humanist scholar, Erasmus of Rotterdam, whom he helped in the preparation of his New Testament in Greek. Warham died at Hackington, a village near Canterbury, in 1532. He was buried in the Martyrdom where his tomb still stands, next to that of Archbishop John Peckham. His portrait by Hans Holbein the younger, painted in 1527, is very probably the first realistic representation of any of the archbishops.

REFORMATION AND COUNTER-REFORMATION: 1532–1558

Thomas Cranmer, who succeeded William Warham in 1533, ranks with Augustine, Anselm and Becket as among the most famed of the Archbishops of Canterbury. His rise to prominence began in 1527 when he was among those who pressed for the solicitation of views from theologians across Europe about the legality of King Henry VIII's marriage to Catherine of Aragon. While in Rome, he met some of the leading figures in the European Reformation and, in January 1532, he became the English ambassador at the court of the Holy Roman Emperor, Charles V.

Cranmer was appointed Archbishop of Canterbury in March 1533, and almost immediately he obliged the King by pronouncing his marriage to Catherine unlawful. Thereafter, he set a theological course that took him increasingly away from Rome and all that it stood for – including the veneration of saints at shrines such as that of St Thomas Becket at Canterbury.

In September 1533, Cranmer baptised Elizabeth, the daughter of the King's second marriage to Anne Boleyn; but Anne's miscarriage of a son in January 1536 was seen by Henry as divine judgement on the marriage and he instructed his chief minister, Thomas Cromwell, to prepare the case for a divorce. Anne was sent to the Tower of London on charges of adultery and incest. Cranmer was reluctant to accept the Queen's guilt, but he was caught up in a royal power game that left him little room for manoeuvre. On 16 May 1536, he visited Anne to hear her confession, and on the following day he formally pronounced her marriage to Henry null and void. When Anne was executed three days later, Cranmer was one of the few to mourn her passing.

Following the death in 1537 of Henry's third wife, Jane Seymour, Cranmer officiated at the King's next marriage to Anne of Cleves, but it remained unconsummated and soon ended in divorce. It cost Cromwell his head, but his execution in July 1540 now left Cranmer in a position of considerable influence with the King and allowed him to press on with his plans for reform. By the time Henry died in 1547, Cranmer had gone a long way towards revising the prayers and liturgies of the English Church, aligning them more closely with the new Protestantism that was sweeping across Europe. It is even said that, instead of administering the last rites at Henry's deathbed, Cranmer read a statement of his proposed reforms.

Buoyed by the Protestant zeal of Henry's successor, his young son Edward VI, Cranmer was now able to press on rapidly with his agenda. He corresponded with many of the influential European reformers and took a leading role in compiling a new Book of Common Prayer, aimed at providing an English liturgy for the Church. The prayer book, which became compulsory in services throughout England in 1549, explicitly rebutted a number of key Roman Catholic doctrines including the transubstantiation of the elements and the authority of the papacy. Three years later, in an extensively revised version that further distanced the English Church from Rome, the traditional prayers for the dead were excluded, thus consigning purgatory to the dustbin of theological dogma.

RIGHT: Thomas Cranmer, Canterbury Cathedral, Chapter House, 19th century

By the early summer of 1553, it was clear that King Edward was dying, and in his will, he named his once-removed Protestant cousin, Jane Grey, as his successor. Cranmer backed Jane's claim to the crown against that of Edward's half-sister, the Catholic Mary Tudor and, in July 1553, Jane was proclaimed queen by her supporters. Almost immediately, however, support for her began to leach away as Mary gathered her forces in East Anglia. In August, Mary rode triumphantly into London on a wave of popular support and was crowned queen – not by Cranmer but by the Bishop of Winchester, Stephen Gardiner. Jane Grey was imprisoned in the Tower of London and later executed, together with her principal supporters.

Mary regarded Cranmer's support for Jane as seditious, and he too went straight to the Tower. In November 1553, he was tried for treason, found guilty and condemned to death, but the sentence was not carried out. In March 1554 he, together with Bishops Hugh Latimer and Nicholas Ridley, were transferred to a prison in Oxford where they were tried for heresy in September 1555. Found guilty, Latimer and Ridley were burnt at the stake in the centre of Oxford. Cranmer's own fate was sealed three months later when Pope Julius III deprived him of the archbishopric of Canterbury and gave permission for the secular authorities to carry out their sentence of death. But then, in what appeared to be his final days, Cranmer wrote several signed recantations of his Protestant faith and embraced the doctrines and liturgy of the Catholic Church that he had so assiduously abjured. He received sacramental absolution and was admitted to the mass.

Under canon law, that should have been enough to save him, but Mary was determined to make an example of the Archbishop and she ordered his execution to proceed. Cranmer was given one last chance to recant, this time in public at a service in the University church in Oxford in March 1556. But in a wholly unexpected act of defiance, he renounced all the recantations he had earlier signed, declaring that the sinful hand that had written them would be the first part of him to be consigned to the flames. He was pulled from the pulpit and dragged to the place where, six months earlier, Latimer and Ridley had met their fiery ends. As the flames rose, Cranmer bravely plunged his right

RIGHT: Thomas Cranmer, Canterbury Cathedral, Chapter House, 19th century

FAR RIGHT: Martyrs' memorial in St Giles, Oxford where Cranmer, Ridley and Latimer were burnt to death in 1555–56

hand into the heart of the fire while declaring that he could see the heavens opening and Jesus standing at the right hand of God, waiting to receive him. He was the fourth Archbishop of Canterbury (after Alphege, Becket and Sudbury) to die a violent death – but he was not to be the last.

Having disposed of Thomas Cranmer, Mary now needed a Catholic archbishop to replace him. Her choice fell upon Reginald Pole, a great-nephew of the last Plantagenet kings, Edward IV and Richard III. A sensitive and intelligent man, Pole graduated from Oxford in 1515 and took part in the sounding out of European theological opinion about the annulment of Henry VIII's marriage to Catherine of Aragon. The King offered him the sees of either York or Winchester in return for his support, but Pole rejected the bribe and went into self-imposed exile on the continent. Although his relationship with Henry was now fractured beyond repair, he prospered in the cauldron of European Catholicism, taking a cardinal's cap in 1536 and attending the opening of the Council of Trent in 1544. Following Mary Tudor's accession to the throne in 1553, Pole returned to England as papal legate and in 1556 he was appointed Archbishop of Canterbury.

As the Queen's chief minister as well as her archbishop, Pole was obliged to support her brutal policy of burning Protestants, though there is evidence that he may privately have wished for a more lenient approach. But as Mary's reign progressed, the people began to turn against her – and also, by association, against Pole. Many who had been indifferent to the English Reformation now began to bridle against the new Catholicism, and the executions that were later to be exalted in John Foxe's *Book of Martyrs* merely stoked the public's revulsion at what they were seeing.

With Mary's relatively early death in November 1558 and the accession of her Protestant half-sister Queen Elizabeth I, Pole's position as Archbishop of Canterbury could now have been precarious; it was not to be, for he died – entirely coincidentally – a mere twelve hours after Mary. There is a popular story that, as he lay on his deathbed in Lambeth Palace, he heard the cheers of the people ringing out for the new queen. It was the end of Roman Catholicism as the established religion of England, and Reginald Pole's destiny was to become the last Roman Catholic Archbishop of Canterbury. However, he is not forgotten, for his plain tomb, surmounted by a shield depicting his family's coat of arms beneath a cardinal's cap, still stands discreetly on the north side of the Corona in Canterbury Cathedral. It bears the simple Latin inscription: *Depositum Cardinalis Poli.*

THE ELIZABETHAN ARCHBISHOPS: 1559–1604

The break from Roman Catholicism that was begun by Henry VIII reached its conclusion in the reign of his daughter, Queen Elizabeth I. The effect upon the governance of the Church was far-reaching. Rome no longer had any say in the appointment of bishops, and in former monastic communities such as Canterbury, the voices of the monks had fallen silent. It was now the Queen – as the supreme head of the Reformed Church of England – who combined in one person the powers and patronage that had previously been divided between the monarchy and the papacy. With her hands now firmly on the levers of ecclesiastical power, Elizabeth became increasingly adept at moving them to her own, and the country's, advantage.

During her long reign of forty-four years, Elizabeth all but saw out three Archbishops of Canterbury: Matthew Parker, Edmund Grindal and John Whitgift. Parker came to Canterbury with a solid portfolio of Protestant credentials: he had been the favourite chaplain of Elizabeth's mother, Anne Boleyn, and he had suffered the loss of several appointments under Mary Tudor. He was not, however, among the groups of English Protestants who chose to spend the few years of Mary's reign in exile abroad.

Parker's installation as Archbishop of Canterbury in December 1559 was the first to be done without reference to Rome, and it therefore raised legal as well as ecclesiastical issues. In the end, it was arranged by a committee of senior canon lawyers and presided over by four English bishops who had themselves been consecrated within the Roman Pontifical – a crucially important detail that allowed the Church of England to claim that its bishops had legitimately been consecrated within the apostolic succession.

From Elizabeth's viewpoint, Parker turned out to be an ideal choice of archbishop to launch her 'middle way' for the Church. He was a man of genuine piety and irreproachable morals, but he was a reluctant innovator and a somewhat uninspiring leader. This was, however, a time when it was more important to consolidate the legacy of Thomas Cranmer than to push the Church into new and unknown territory, and Parker proved himself capable of suppressing Catholicism in most parts of the country while facing down the clamant demands of Puritans and dissenters. However, he never gained the wholehearted support of the Queen, and she never admitted him to her Privy Council. In any case, Elizabeth had a strong prejudice against married clergy and was said positively to have disliked Parker's wife, Margaret.

Although not regarded as a scholar of the first rank, Parker left some important theological legacies, prominent among them the Thirty-Nine Articles of Religion of 1562 that set out the foundational doctrines of the Church of England. He also oversaw the introduction of the so-called Bishops' Bible, which was published at his own expense in 1572. In his will, he bequeathed a priceless collection of historical manuscripts to Corpus Christi College in Cambridge, among them the Gospels of St Augustine and an 11th-century psalter that may once have belonged to Alphege and Becket.

RIGHT: Queen Elizabeth I, by George Gower, 1588

VINCIT QVI PATITVR

Æ 68

EDMVNDVS GRINDALVS
CANTVAR. ARCHIEPS.
Anno Domini. 1580
Ætatis Suæ. 61.

De Vos.

ABOVE: **Edmund Grindal**, artist uknown

LEFT: **John Whitgift**, artist unknown

When Matthew Parker died in May 1575, he was succeeded by the unworldly and impeccably unmarried Edmund Grindal. Like Parker, Grindal had started his ecclesiastical career in the royal court where he was a chaplain to Edward VI, and in 1553 he was nominated Bishop of London. However, Edward died before the appointment could be made and Mary Tudor had no time for him. He left England during the Marian period, joining a group of Protestant exiles in Strasbourg where Cranmer's 1552 prayer book was in use. Grindal returned to England on the day of Queen Elizabeth's coronation in January 1559 when he finally secured the bishopric of London. He was promoted to be Archbishop of York in 1570 and of Canterbury five years later.

As archbishop, Grindal fell out rather spectacularly with the Queen, who wanted him to take a tougher stand against Puritanism. She particularly urged him to suppress the spread of 'prophesyings' – regular meetings at which clergymen, commonly with Puritan leanings, expounded and discussed the scriptures. In 1577 Elizabeth issued an order prohibiting any further prophesyings, and she required Grindal to report any uncooperative clergy. He refused, explaining his reasons to the Queen in a defiantly lengthy letter. Elizabeth responded by suspending him from his jurisdictional (though not his spiritual) functions as archbishop, and he was more or less confined to house arrest for the majority of his time as archbishop. In 1582, however, he apologised to the Queen and his full archiepiscopal authority was restored, but by then it was almost too late. In 1583 he drafted a resignation letter but died at the archbishop's palace at Croydon before it could be put into effect. He was buried in the parish church there.

The third of Queen Elizabeth's archbishops was John Whitgift who, until his appointment to Canterbury in 1583, had been deeply involved in the academic and administrative life of Cambridge University. Having matriculated at Queen's College in 1549, he moved first to Pembroke Hall and then to Peterhouse before taking holy orders in 1560 and becoming chaplain to the Bishop of Ely, Richard Cox.

Whitgift returned to Cambridge in 1563 as Lady Margaret Professor of Divinity. He then served as master of Pembroke Hall and Trinity College before becoming vice-chancellor of the university in 1570.

During his twenty years as archbishop, Whitgift's relationship with the Queen was relaxed and co-operative. Instinctively obedient to those in authority, he supported Elizabeth's policy of religious uniformity in the Church of England and he threw himself into the acrimonious struggle to secure the passage of the Act Against Seditious Sectaries in 1593, which made Puritanism an offence. He was, however, mistrusted by some of the Queen's closest advisers, including Leicester and Walsingham, who thought his views too rigid and felt he was going too far in seeking out Puritan sympathisers among the clergy. Whitgift attended Elizabeth on her deathbed in March 1603 and later in the year he crowned her successor, the Scottish James Stuart, as King James I of England.

Shortly before his death in January 1604, Whitgift attended the Hampton Court Conference, a meeting between the new King and his bishops to consider the Millenary Petition – a set of demands, said to have been signed by a hundred Puritan ministers, reflecting their belief that reform in the English Church had not gone far enough. James handled the conference with skill, managing to accommodate some of the Puritans' demands without overly upsetting the Anglican hierarchy. The most enduring outcome of the Conference was the initiation of a process that culminated in 1611 with the publication of the King James Bible. Properly known as the Authorised Version because it was the only one allowed to be read in Anglican churches, it remains one of the supreme achievements of English literary scholarship.

John Whitgift died at Lambeth Palace a few weeks after the Hampton Court Conference and was buried at Croydon. His death may have come as something of a setback for King James, as Whitgift's successor – Richard Bancroft – had zealously opposed the Puritan demands at Hampton Court and was just as committed to attacking them from the pulpit at Canterbury. James may well have felt that he could do without such sectarian infighting as he sought to keep the religious life of his new kingdom on an even keel.

RIGHT: Coat of arms of George Abbot, Canterbury Cathedral, Library Corridor, circa 17th century

THE RISING TIDE OF PURITANISM: 1604–1645

Richard Bancroft was born in Lancashire in 1544, educated at Cambridge and ordained priest in about 1570. In 1589 he delivered a fiercely anti-Puritan sermon at St Paul's Cross, London, in which he proclaimed the divine right of bishops – a favourite target for Puritan ire – in such strong and passionate language that one of Queen Elizabeth's councillors thought it almost an attempt to undermine her position as the supreme head of the Church. It evidently did Bancroft no harm, however, for in 1597 he was consecrated Bishop of London. John Whitgift, the Archbishop of Canterbury at the time, was one of his sponsors, but by now Whitgift was in failing health and Bancroft took on some of his duties. Both were present at the deathbed of Elizabeth in March 1603. In the following January, Bancroft attended the Hampton Court Conference. At first, he appeared to be sympathetic towards the Millenary Petition, but following his installation as Archbishop of Canterbury in November 1604, he reverted to type and adopted a much tougher line towards Puritanism. However, he survived for only six years as archbishop, dying at Lambeth in November 1610.

Richard Bancroft was succeeded in 1611 by his nominee, George Abbot, who was born in Guildford in 1562 and educated at the Royal Grammar School there. He studied and then taught at Oxford before becoming Dean of Winchester in 1600 and Bishop of London in 1610. Described by one of his contemporaries as 'a man of strong principles but narrow outlook', Abbot held a high view of Anglicanism, insisting that – in spite of the break with Rome – its priests and bishops had been canonically consecrated within the apostolic succession. In doing so, he had to face down a popular fiction of the time, known as the Nag's Head fable, which claimed that Matthew Parker's installation as archbishop in 1559 had amounted to nothing more than having a Bible pressed to his neck at a makeshift ceremony in the Nag's Head tavern in Cheapside. To lay the fable to rest, Abbot invited a number of senior Roman Catholics to study the actual circumstances of Parker's installation, and they duly pronounced them satisfactory. It was an important moment for the Church of England.

In spite of his high-church view of the episcopacy, Abbot had a degree of sympathy with Puritanism that brought him into conflict with King James I. In 1618 he opposed the Declaration of Sports, a royally-approved list of games and recreations that were permitted after divine service on Sundays (including archery and Morris dancing but not bowling or bear-baiting), and he further incurred the King's displeasure by opposing the divorce petition of the scandalous Lady Frances Howard against her husband Robert Devereux, the Earl of Essex. Complementing Abbot's moderate sympathy for Puritanism was his sometimes harsh treatment of Catholics – a stance that brought him into direct conflict with the King over the projected marriage of the Prince of Wales (later King Charles I) to the Spanish Infanta, Maria Anna.

In a bizarre accident in 1621, Abbot became the subject of a damaging scandal while hunting on Lord Zouch's estate in Hampshire. An arrow aimed at a deer accidently hit a servant, Peter Hawkins, who died within the hour. Although it was not seen as anything other than a tragic

RIGHT: William Laud, by Sir Anthony Van Dyke, circa 1636

accident, Abbot's Catholic enemies pointedly observed that hunting was not a sport in which an archbishop should have been engaging in the first place. Such was the prominence given to the incident that the King referred it to a commission of enquiry and Abbot was relieved of some of his public duties. He did, however, attend James I in his last illness in 1625 and in the following year, he crowned his successor, Charles I, as King of England, Ireland and Scotland. Abbot soon fell out with Charles over his arrogant and autocratic manner, and in 1627, the King suspended him from his duties. As a result, the de facto leadership of the Church passed to the Bishop of London, William Laud, and the last four years of Abbot's period in office were ones of semi-retirement.

George Abbot died at his archiepiscopal palace at Croydon in August 1633 and was buried in his native town of Guildford. Almost inevitably, he was succeeded by the arch-Royalist Laud. Laud was born in 1573, educated at Oxford and ordained priest in 1601. In spite of enjoying the confidence of one of James I's prominent favourites, George Villiers, Laud had an uneven relationship with the King, and his career stuttered. The best he managed to achieve in James's reign was the relatively lowly bishopric of St David's, but when James died in 1625 and was succeeded by his son, King Charles I, Laud's fortunes changed and he rose rapidly through the ranks. In 1626, he succeeded Lancelot Andrewes as Dean of the Chapel Royal, and two years later he became Bishop of London. He was close to Charles in 1629 when the King began his personal rule without recourse to parliament, and he was installed as Archbishop of Canterbury four years later.

A fierce opponent of Puritanism, Laud arrived in Canterbury with a clear commitment to order and discipline in the Church of England. He regarded the formality and dignity of worship – based upon the twin foundations of the Scriptures and the Creeds – as the supreme expression of the Christian faith, and he was harsh on those who opposed him. His most obstinate critic was the Bishop of Lincoln, John Williams, whose liberal attitudes towards Puritanism led to his indictment in the Star Chamber in 1636 on a charge of conspiracy to commit perjury. He was found guilty and imprisoned in the Tower of London. Under pressure from Puritan sympathisers in the aristocracy, he was released by Charles I in 1640 and in the following year he was appointed Archbishop of York

Williams now began agitating for the impeachment of Laud, claiming that he was covertly sympathetic towards Catholicism – a claim that he knew would go down well among the rising tide of Puritanism. Swayed in part by Williams's antipathy towards Laud, the King finally lost

ABOVE: **William Laud, Canterbury Cathedral, Chapter House, 19th century**

patience with his archbishop, believing him now to be a source of damaging dissension within the Church. Not having committed any indictable offence, Laud's arrest in 1641 on a charge of treason was largely a politically motivated act by a parliament that had long been treated dismissively by him. He was held in the Tower of London where he remained throughout the early stages of the English Civil War.

When Laud was finally brought to trial in 1644, nothing of treasonable substance could be proved against him, and the trial ended without a verdict. In the following year (1645), the Long Parliament abandoned the possibility of any legal solution by passing a bill of attainder – a legislative device that allowed a finding of guilt without the need for a trial. Laud was granted a royal pardon, but it failed to save him and, still protesting his innocence, he was executed on Tower Hill in January 1645. He was buried first at the nearby church of All Hallows by the Tower, but after the restoration of the monarchy in 1660, his body was removed to the chapel of St John's College, Oxford.

LEFT: Execution of William Laud on Tower Hill in 1645, Canterbury Cathedral, Chapter House, 20th century

REGICIDE, RESTORATION AND A GLORIOUS REVOLUTION: 1645–1693

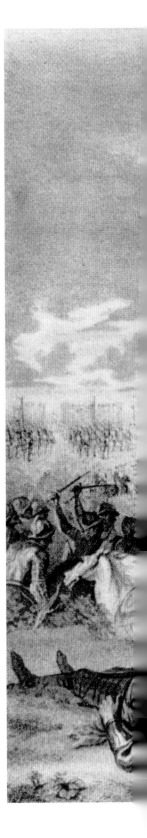

Following the execution of William Laud in 1645, the Archbishop's Throne at Canterbury remained vacant for fifteen years. With the outbreak of Civil War in 1642, the Long Parliament remained in session, but it was now dominated by Puritans who saw the whole system of Church governance as a corrupt legacy of the old Catholicism. Broadly speaking, Puritanism divided into two loosely separate groups: Presbyterians, who agitated for a non-hierarchical form of Church governance, and Independents, most of whom demanded nothing less than the complete separation of Church and State. The issue of religion in general and the fate of Anglicanism in particular now became a major preoccupation for parliament, and in 1643 the Westminster Assembly was convened to consider the future of the Church of England. Consisting mainly of theologians and parliamentarians, the Assembly was markedly Calvinist in outlook and based its deliberations upon the (by now) time-hallowed Protestant belief in the Bible as the authoritative word of God. Many of the Assembly's recommendations were acted upon, including the replacement of the Book of Common Prayer with a Directory of Worship in 1645 and the exclusion of bishops from the Church of England a year later. The timing was propitious: Laud was now out of the way; the Archbishop of York had been placed under virtual house arrest, and most of the other bishops had taken early retirement.

Without bishops, and with deans and chapters already having stood down, the cathedrals lost most of their raisons d'être – and, in the case of Canterbury, much of its material splendour as well. In August 1642 the parliamentarian Colonel Edwin Sandys entered the cathedral with his troops and proceeded to despoil or seize a large number of religious artefacts. A few months later a great deal of the medieval stained glass was destroyed by the Reverend Dick Culmer, a Puritan clergyman who, as a commissioner under Oliver Cromwell, was charged with demolishing whatever 'superstitious' artefacts had managed to survive. Little is known about the cathedral in the wake of these destructive purges. The building was taken over by Presbyterian squatters for their Sunday services and sermons were preached in the Chapter House; but any semblance of normal cathedral life was put on hold until the restoration of the monarchy in 1660 and the appointment of William Juxon as the first Restoration Archbishop of Canterbury.

Juxon was educated at the Merchant Taylors School in London and Oxford University. He was on good terms with William Laud, whose election as Archbishop of Canterbury he had

RIGHT: The victory at Naseby of Cromwell's Parliamentarian New Model Army in 1645

helped to secure, and he was acceptable to King Charles I who appointed him chaplain-in-ordinary. Thereafter his rise was swift: Dean of Worcester in 1627, Bishop of London in 1633, and Lord Treasurer in 1636. Juxon remained close to Charles throughout the Civil War and administered the last rites to him on the scaffold before his execution in Whitehall in 1649. Some attribute to him the prophetic words of martyrdom as the axe came down: 'You are exchanged from a temporal to an eternal crown, a good exchange.'

Shortly afterwards, Juxon was deprived of the bishopric of London and he retired to his estate in Gloucestershire for the duration of the Commonwealth where he attended to his hounds; but following the accession of King Charles II in 1660, he was summoned from retirement and, at the age of seventy-eight, appointed Archbishop of Canterbury. Shortly after taking part in Charles's coronation service, however, Juxon's health began to fail and he died at Lambeth in June 1663. He was buried at St John's College Oxford, whither the remains of William Laud were shortly to be transferred.

William Juxon was succeeded by Gilbert Sheldon, who was born in Staffordshire towards the end of Queen Elizabeth's reign in 1598. He was educated at both Oxford and Cambridge, and from 1632 to 1639 he held livings in London, Oxfordshire and Buckinghamshire. When the Civil War broke out in 1642, Sheldon, who had no Puritan sympathies at all, became acquainted with many Royalist leaders and was for a time a chaplain to Charles I; but, perforce, he had chosen the wrong side. When Oxford fell to the Parliamentarians in 1646 he was taken into custody and placed under what amounted to house arrest in the East Midlands, where he was active in raising funds for Charles's son, the heir apparent.

Sheldon got his predictable reward when the monarchy was restored in 1660. He was appointed Bishop of London in October of that year and Archbishop of Canterbury in the wake of Juxon's death in the summer of 1663. Four years later, he became de facto Chancellor of Oxford University, a post to which he devoted much time and money. The Sheldonian Theatre in Oxford is his most visible legacy, but Sheldon also left a less tangible record of probity and service during his time as the second Restoration Archbishop. He dealt sensibly with the major issues that came his way, reproved Charles II for his philandering and remained in London at the height of the plague in 1665 to give spiritual comfort to its victims. A man of 'undoubted piety' (according to his chaplain), he regarded the principal purpose of religion as 'the practice of a good life'. Samuel Pepys praised him as 'a stout and spirited man' who 'spoke his mind'.

Gilbert Sheldon died at Lambeth in November 1677 and was buried at Croydon. He was succeeded in the following year by William Sancroft, a gentle and pious man who was uncomfortable in the spotlight of national politics. Born in Suffolk in 1617, Sancroft became a fellow of Emmanuel College, Cambridge but was thrown out in 1651 for refusing to accept the Oath of Engagement, a declaration of loyalty to the Commonwealth that was binding upon those in public life. Sancroft had little choice but to leave England. With the accession of Charles II in 1660, however, he was brought back from exile to become Dean of St Paul's. While there he witnessed Old St Paul's destroyed in the Great Fire of London in 1666, a tragedy that he blamed on the licentiousness of the age and that he used as an opportunity to call for a period of national repentance. Following the fire Sancroft negotiated with Christopher Wren to design a 'handsome and noble' replacement, chipping in £1,400 of his own money towards the cost.

RIGHT: William Sancroft, artist unknown

Sancroft was appointed Archbishop of Canterbury in 1678, in which capacity he attended Charles II on his deathbed in 1685 and later crowned Charles's Catholic brother, James II. But Sancroft had little sympathy for the new King, and he refused to accept the Declaration of Indulgence, a decree promulgated by James that allowed a greater freedom of worship. Perceiving a threat to their own monopoly – quite apart from opening the floodgates to all manner of objectionable religious practices, including Catholic ones – many Anglican clergy refused to read the declaration in their churches; and, led by Sancroft, a group of bishops petitioned the King to withdraw it. Furious at what he saw as their rebelliousness, James committed them to the Tower of London and ordered them to be tried for seditious libel. In a verdict that was disastrous for the Catholic King, they were found not guilty and acquitted.

Sancroft's reprieve was, however, short-lived for, following the Glorious Revolution in 1688 that saw James cast into exile and brought King William III and Queen Mary II to the throne, he was suspended in 1690 for refusing to take the Oath of Allegiance to the new monarchs. Along with many of the clergy, he felt bound by his previous oath to James II, which he could not break while the former King was still alive. Following his suspension, Sancroft's archiepiscopal duties were taken over by the Dean of St Paul's, John Tillotson, in anticipation of his own appointment as archbishop in the following year. William Sancroft retired to his native village of Fressingfield, in Suffolk, where he died in November 1693 and where he was buried.

LEFT: Old St Paul's Cathedral destroyed by fire in 1666, from *A First Book of English History*, 1925

THE LATER STUART AND EARLY HANOVERIAN ARCHBISHOPS: 1690–1758

The reluctant successor to William Sancroft as Archbishop of Canterbury was John Tillotson, the Dean of St Paul's at the time of his election. Tillotson had taken on much of Sancroft's work after he was suspended in 1690 for refusing to take the Oath of Allegiance to King William and Queen Mary, but he had grave reservations about his promotion to Canterbury, fearing that he might become the wedge that would finally drive Sancroft into the ecclesiastical wilderness. To accommodate his misgivings, his enthronement as archbishop was delayed until the spring of 1691; once in office, he was appreciated for his intelligence, warm-heartedness and liberal outlook. After his death in 1694, he was found to have been giving a fifth of his income to charity, leaving his widow almost penniless.

Tillotson was more ecumenical in outlook than many of his predecessors. He was born into a Puritan family in Yorkshire in 1630 and was taken at first to be a Presbyterian, but when the Act of Uniformity became law in 1662, he switched his allegiance to Anglicanism and, having by now been ordained priest, accepted livings in Hertfordshire and Suffolk. However, throughout his ministry he retained a measure of sympathy towards non-conformists and even Catholics: he once remarked that while papism was 'gross superstition', papists were 'doubtless made like other men'.

In 1664 Tillotson married Elizabeth French, a niece of Oliver Cromwell, and in 1672 he became Dean of Canterbury. Following the coronation of William and Mary in 1689, Tillotson enjoyed the confidence of the royals and was appointed Clerk of the Closet, an ecclesiastical preferment created in the 15th century to advise the monarch on suitable candidates for royal chaplaincies. He moved from the deanship of Canterbury to that of St Paul's in 1689, returning to Canterbury as archbishop in May 1691. Tillotson was noted for the clarity and rationality of his sermons, but he made enemies through his attempts at Church reform, especially over the vexed issue of priests who were habitually absent from their parishes. The stress that this caused him was thought to have hastened his end, and he died in November 1694 after only three years as primate. He was buried in the church of St Lawrence Jewry in the City of London.

John Tillotson was succeeded by Thomas Tenison, who was born into good Anglican stock in Cambridgeshire in 1636. A large, brawny figure, strong in his youth but afflicted with gout in later life, Tenison was ordained priest in 1659 and was appointed an upper minister of St Peter Mancroft in Norwich in 1670. Ten years later he moved to St Martin's in the Fields where he preached a controversial sermon at Nell Gwynn's funeral in 1687 on the theme of the great joy in heaven over a repentant sinner. An uncompromising opponent of Catholicism, Tenison found himself locked in almost perpetual conflict with King James II, his near-neighbour at the Palace of Whitehall (not yet destroyed by fire), who dismissed him as a 'dull man' with a 'languid oration'.

RIGHT: Clockwise from top left: John Tillotson, after Sir Godfrey Kneller; Thomas Tenison, by Robert White; John Potter, after Thomas Hudson; William Wake, by Thomas Gibson

With the accession of William and Mary, however, his fortunes changed. He was appointed Bishop of Lincoln in 1691, and three years later he was enthroned as Archbishop of Canterbury – the first such ceremony in the cathedral since the Reformation.

As archbishop, Tenison attended both Mary and William on their deathbeds in 1694 and 1702 respectively, and he crowned William's successor, Queen Anne, but he found little favour in her court, where he was seen as too low-church. His political influence drained away during the last years of Anne's reign, and the coronation of George I at Westminster Abbey in 1714 was almost his last public act. Tenison's death in the following year marked a turning point in the history of English politics. For a thousand years until the early 18th century it had been almost impossible to describe the governance of the country without reference to the English Church and its senior archbishop. With the arrival of the Hanoverians, however, a sea-change began to take place in the political landscape as power shifted away from the Church towards a resurgent parliament. The days of the archbishopric of Canterbury as a potent political force in a secular state were draining away, never to return.

Thomas Tenison was succeeded by William Wake, whose career was entirely unremarkable. Born in Dorset and educated at Oxford University, Wake was successively a canon of Oxford, rector of St James Westminster, Dean of Exeter and Bishop of Lincoln. He was appointed Archbishop of Canterbury on the death of Tenison and he died at Lambeth in 1737. His twenty-two years as archbishop are remembered mainly for a rather obscure and ultimately unsuccessful plan to establish inter-communion between the Church of England and the Gallican Church in France – a nominally Catholic sect whose members held the distinctly uncatholic belief that, because kings were anointed directly by God, they could not be subject to the Pope. The project collapsed, and Wake spent much of his time thereafter writing well-received historical works. Following his death in 1737, he was buried at Croydon.

The next Archbishop of Canterbury was John Potter, a Yorkshireman who was born into a non-conformist family in about 1674. After ordination in 1698, he served as chaplain to both Archbishop Thomas Tenison and Queen Anne until his appointment in 1708 as Regius Professor of Divinity at Oxford University. With it came a canon's stall at Oxford Cathedral and, in 1715, the bishopric of Oxford. A noted Whig, Potter's appointment to Canterbury in 1737 was unexpected, but he had always pursued a high-church line, thereby endearing himself to the Hanoverians. Once in office, however, Potter seems to have drawn upon his non-conformist background to reach out to other Christian sects. He met the influential Moravian count, Nicholas Zinzendorf, and as the Bishop of Oxford who had earlier ordained John and Charles Wesley into the Anglican ministry, he was well disposed towards the fledgling Methodist Church.

John Potter died of an apoplectic fit in 1747 and was buried at Croydon. His successor, Thomas Herring, had a career trajectory very similar to that of many of his predecessors. He was educated at Cambridge, became a fellow of Corpus Christi College, and served as chaplain to King George II. Further promotions followed: the bishopric of Bangor in 1737, the archbishopric of York in 1743, and the archbishopric of Canterbury in 1747. It was during Herring's time at York that the Jacobite rising of 1745 erupted, and Herring – a loyal Hanoverian – preached a rousing sermon on the theme of patriotism and Protestantism that elicited the fulsome approval of Horace Walpole and the grateful thanks of the King.

Once in office at Canterbury, however, Herring seems largely to have run out of steam. This was a time when the Church of England was in the doldrums, lacking in life and energy, and the religious fervour of the nation was being stirred not by establishment figures like Herring but

RIGHT: Thomas Herring,
by William Hogarth, 1744

by popular revivalist preachers such as the Wesley brothers and George Whitefield. Evangelical non-conformism was emerging from the closet, and Herring seemed at a loss to know how to respond – other than, perhaps, by underscoring the eminence of his own position. The famous portrait of him by Hogarth, painted in 1744, shows a man of supreme self-satisfaction, looking down upon the viewer from his throne as though untroubled by the tumultuous events swirling around him. Indeed, in a letter to his friend William Duncombe, Herring rejoiced that he had been 'called up to this high station at a time when spite, and rancour, and bitterness of spirit are out of countenance [and] we breathe the benign and comfortable air of liberty and toleration'. It was a suitable epitaph for him.

When Thomas Herring died in 1757 he was succeeded for a brief time by Matthew Hutton, a high-churchman who came to Canterbury having previously been a chaplain to King George II and a canon of Windsor. Hutton followed in Herring's footsteps as Bishop of Bangor, Archbishop of York and finally Archbishop of Canterbury, but he was in office for less than a year and he never got to live in Lambeth Palace – largely, it seems, because it was more or less uninhabitable at the time. He died in March 1758 and was buried in the chapel at Lambeth.

ANGLICANISM IN THE COLONIES: 1758–1848

By the time Thomas Secker succeeded Matthew Hutton as Archbishop of Canterbury in 1758, the future of the American colonies was at the forefront of political and ecclesiastical concerns in Britain. The Church of England had had a presence in America since the founding of Jamestown in 1607 and, as it spread through the colonies, it came loosely under the jurisdiction of the Bishop of London; the American clergy were now agitating for a bishop of their own. They found themselves opposed by the vested interests of churchmen and settlers who foresaw their liberties eroding if Anglicanism in America became an episcopal Church under the authority of Lambeth. By the mid-18th century, the issue had reached something of a crisis. Archbishop Secker threw his authority behind the case for an American episcopacy, but his intervention merely fed the simmering resentment of many colonists who saw it as an ill-disguised attempt to shore up a deeply unpopular government through the back door of Anglican imperialism.

At home, Secker has been seen as a model of 18th-century Anglican orthodoxy. He was much respected as a pastor and administrator who before his promotion to Canterbury had been rector of St James's Piccadilly, Bishop of Oxford and Bishop of Bristol. A favourite of King George III, whom he baptised, crowned and married, Secker was the recipient of a miniature portrait given to him by the King in 1761 as a token of his esteem. Like many high-church Anglicans of his time, he had a horror of 'enthusiasm' and he held grave reservations about the progress that Methodism was making under the evangelical zeal of the Wesley brothers – though he did nothing deliberately to hinder their mission. Secker died at Lambeth in August 1768 and was buried in a covered passage leading from the palace to the church.

Thomas Secker was succeeded by Frederick Cornwallis, an entirely conventional Georgian churchman who was born into a titled family in 1713 and educated at Eton and Cambridge. Aided in part by his aristocratic connections, Cornwallis rose quickly in the Church, becoming chaplain to King George II, Bishop of Lichfield and Dean of St Paul's. As Archbishop of Canterbury, Cornwallis was liked for his sociability – even his geniality – but he could scarcely be said to have been a decisive leader at a time when the Church of England was facing the possibility of extinction in America. He was a loyal supporter of Lord North, upon whom much of the blame for the loss of the American colonies has been heaped, but he did display a genuine concern for clergymen in America who were losing their livelihoods as a result of the War. Cornwallis died in 1783 and was buried at Lambeth.

Frederick Cornwallis's successor, John Moore, was nominated in March 1783. The son of a grazier, Moore was born in 1730 and educated at the free grammar school in Gloucester and Oxford University. Following his ordination, he spent time at Woodstock where he was tutor to the sons of the Duke of Marlborough at nearby Blenheim Palace; and this chance association with the family helped to secure the deanship of Canterbury in 1771 and the bishopric of Bangor four years later. Following the death of Cornwallis in 1783, Moore returned to Canterbury, where he remained as archbishop until his own death in 1805.

RIGHT: **William Howley,** artist unknown

ABᵖ HOWLE
Martin S.

It was during Moore's period in office that the first bishop of the Episcopal Church in the United States, Samuel Seabury, was consecrated. A loyalist during the Revolution, Seabury could not be consecrated in America (as there were not yet any bishops there to carry it out), and he was eventually consecrated as bishop in the Scottish Episcopal Church – an act that raised the alarming prospect of a Jacobite Church in America. In response, parliament made legal provision for the ordination of foreign bishops and, in 1787, Charles Inglis became the first Anglican bishop for the colonies when he was consecrated to the newly formed diocese of Nova Scotia. In the same year, Moore consecrated two further American bishops, Samuel Provoost in Pennsylvania and William White in New York.

Following John Moore's death in 1805, the next Archbishop of Canterbury was Charles Manners Sutton, a grandson of the third Duke of Rutland. He was educated at Charterhouse School and Cambridge and, at the age of twenty-three, he eloped with his cousin, Mary Thoroton, by whom he later had ten daughters and two sons. In 1791 Manners Sutton became Dean of Peterborough and three years later Bishop of Norwich, a position that he held concurrently (*in commendam*) with that of Dean of Windsor. Through the Windsor connection, he had become close to the large family of George III, and it was the king's prerogative that secured Canterbury for him. The prime minister, William Pitt, had wanted to see the Bishop of Lincoln, Sir George Pretyman Tomline, in that office.

As archbishop, Manners Sutton threw his weight behind the revival of Anglicanism in Britain at a time of rapid social and industrial change. He was actively sympathetic to the activities of the National Society, formed to establish schools for the education of poor children, and he energetically supported the (somewhat flagging) Society for Promoting Christian Knowledge. He also campaigned for the establishment of bishops in India, and in 1814 he consecrated Thomas Middleton as the first Bishop of the new diocese of Calcutta. Five years later, in 1819, Manners Sutton christened the future Queen Victoria at Kensington Palace. During his primacy, the old archiepiscopal palace at Croydon was sold and the proceeds used to buy Addington Palace nearby, where he was buried in the parish church after dying at Lambeth in July 1828.

The next to occupy the Archbishop's Throne was another high-churchman, William Howley. Although he was the last Archbishop of Canterbury to be appointed under the Hanoverians, his connections with royalty extended into the Victorian era for, in the early hours of 20 June 1837, he accompanied the Lord Chamberlain, the Marquess of Conyngham, to Kensington Palace to inform the young Princess Victoria of her accession to the throne. Howley crowned Victoria in

ABOVE: The Howley-Harrison Library, Canterbury Cathedral

ABOVE: Bruton parish church, colonial Williamsburg, Virginia

Westminster Abbey in the following year, and in 1840 he conducted her marriage to Prince Albert.

Howley was educated at Winchester and Oxford, and in 1809 he was appointed Regius Professor of Divinity at Oxford and a canon of Christ Church Cathedral. Promotion to the bishopric of London came in 1813 and to Canterbury in 1828. A natural conservative, he was the last Archbishop of Canterbury to wear a wig. As the recently enthroned archbishop, Howley was a member of the House of Lords when three great issues came before parliament: the repeal of the Test and Corporation Acts in 1828, which abolished the requirement for public servants to be communicant members of the Church of England; the Roman Catholic Relief Bill in 1829, which permitted Catholics to sit in parliament, and the Reform Bill in 1832, which introduced far-reaching changes in the electoral system. Howley led a somewhat divided bench of bishops in their opposition to all three measures, and such was his personal antipathy towards the Reform Act that his carriage was attacked in the streets of Canterbury. The citizens of his diocese evidently did not share his horror at upsetting the delicate balance of the British constitution.

Howley was a noted builder who restored Fulham Palace and refashioned the residential areas of Lambeth Palace. His great legacy to Canterbury was the large collection of books that he and his chaplain, Benjamin Harrison, left to the dean and chapter. It forms a large part of what is now the Howley-Harrison Library. William Howley died in 1848 and was buried at Addington. By then, Victoria had been on the throne for eleven years, and the building blocks of the British Empire were being levered into place: no fewer than twelve new bishops were consecrated to British colonies during his archiepiscopate. It was, though, his successors who had to deal with the huge changes that were underway.

HERESY, RITUALISM AND THE PUBLIC SCHOOLS: 1848–1896

When John Bird Sumner succeeded William Howley as Archbishop of Canterbury in 1848, the Oxford Movement had been making waves within the Church of England for some time. John Henry Newman had already converted to Rome and Edward Pusey was adding his own contribution to the flow of pamphlets that gave the movement the soubriquet of Tractarianism. Sumner had little time for these high-church sentiments, preferring the Church to direct its energies towards more practical matters. Sometimes described as the first modern evangelical Archbishop of Canterbury, he was primarily a pastor and only secondarily an ecclesiastical leader – a combination of characteristics that led the Bishop of Oxford, Samuel Wilberforce, to describe him as 'good, gentle, loving and weak'.

Sumner could not, however, entirely ignore the views of the Tractarians and, shortly after his appointment to Canterbury, he was drawn into the controversial case of George Gorham, an Anglican priest who was seeking appointment in the Devon village of Brampford Speke. At one point, Gorham was examined by the Bishop of Exeter, Henry Phillpotts, on his views about baptism. Phillpotts judged his answers to be doctrinally amiss and declined to make the appointment. Gorham then appealed to the Privy Council, which found in his favour. The decision, which Sumner supported, angered many leading members of the Church of England who left to join Rome, and Phillpotts wrote a famously vigorous letter to the Archbishop accusing him of condoning heresy in the Church. Thereafter he declined to have any further communication with Sumner, though he did publicly announce his intention of praying for him as 'an affectionate friend for nearly thirty years and now your afflicted servant'.

On the great social issues of the day, Sumner held broadly progressive views. As Bishop of Chester, he voted in favour of the Reform Bill in the House of Lords in 1832 and, although he was opposed to any major concessions towards Catholicism, he did support the Roman Catholic Relief Bill in 1829. In 1857, as Archbishop of Canterbury, he voted in favour of the Matrimonial Causes Bill, which paved the way for divorce through civil proceedings. On the other hand, Sumner voted against the Jewish Relief Bill in 1858 which, once it became law, allowed Jews to become MPs.

John Bird Sumner died in 1862 and was buried at Addington. He was succeeded by Charles Longley, who was promoted to Canterbury from the archbishopric of York. Longley was born in Kent in 1794 and educated at Westminster School and Oxford. In 1829, at the age of only thirty-five, he was appointed headmaster of Harrow School – the first of a select group of Victorian and Edwardian clergymen who led some of the great English public schools before finishing up as Archbishop of Canterbury. Longley was consecrated Bishop of the new diocese of Ripon in 1836 and of Durham in 1856. He was promoted to York in 1860, a position that he held for two years before his preferment to Canterbury.

RIGHT: Charles Longley, artist unknown

Longley's abiding legacy to the Church of England was the first Lambeth Conference, convened in September 1867 and attended by seventy-eight British, Colonial and American bishops. Although a good deal of routine business was conducted at the Conference, it was dominated by the crisis over the Bishop of Natal, John Colenso. Drawing on his missionary experiences in preaching to native Africans, Colenso realised that much of what had passed for centuries as mainstream Christian teaching in the West was simply unintelligible to his African congregations, cutting right across the ancient beliefs and practices of their communities. From this starting point, Colenso fashioned a Christian defence of polygamy and he refused to preach about eternal damnation. He also felt unable to commend parts of the Bible as the literal word of God. Such actions created a frenzy of alarm among high-churchmen in both South Africa and England, and Colenso was removed from office by the Bishop of Cape Town, Robert Gray. Upon appeal, the Privy Council ruled that the dismissal had been illegal. Although the Archbishop personally regarded Colenso's opinions as heretical, Longley refused to allow a motion to be put to the Lambeth Conference that, if passed, would have condemned him. The episode raised difficult questions for the Conference not just about doctrine but also the extent of Lambeth's jurisdiction in the colonies. They were questions that were to linger for a long time.

Charles Longley died in October 1868 and was succeeded by Archibald Campbell Tait, a Scotsman who became one of the foremost public figures of his day. Tait was born into a Presbyterian family in Edinburgh in 1811 and was educated at the Universities of Glasgow and Oxford. As a fellow of Balliol College, he encountered the Oxford Movement at first hand and rejected both its creeds and the mysticism in which it wrapped itself. Indeed, when Newman published his famous tract XC in 1841 defending the Articles of Religion as wholly compatible with the authentic teaching of the Catholic Church, it was Tait who led the protest of a group of Oxford fellows against it.

Tait was appointed headmaster of Rugby School in 1842 in succession to the celebrated Dr Thomas Arnold, but he had had no experience of English public schools and his time there was undistinguished. From Rugby, he went to the deanery of Carlisle where he experienced the overwhelming tragedy of losing five of his six daughters to scarlet fever in the space of five weeks. The insight that this gave him into the nature of suffering was to have a profound effect on his Christian faith and ministry. From Carlisle, Tait became Bishop of London in 1856 and Archbishop of Canterbury in 1868.

Tait's time as archbishop was dominated by the Anglo-Catholic revival in the Church of England, particularly the vexed question of ritualism, which sought to bring elements of Roman Catholic worship into mainstream Anglican practice. They included the use of eucharistic vestments, the placing of candles on the high altar, and the mixing of sacramental wine with water. Tait believed that people were generally opposed to these kinds of rituals so, in 1874, he introduced a Private Member's bill into the House of Lords (the Public Worship Regulation Bill) to stamp it out. After the bill became law, a number of prominent clergymen who refused to accept it were imprisoned for contempt of court – conscientious ritualists turned into martyrs by the law of the land. Some regard it as Tait's greatest mistake.

In the long run, however, Tait is remembered more for his pastoral work than for his involvement in Church politics. As Bishop of London, he had encouraged his clergy to engage with the everyday circumstances of people's lives, and he himself preached open-air sermons to immigrants, cab drivers, porters, fruiterers, fishmongers and anyone else who would listen to him. Thanks to his common touch, afternoon services in many London churches were packed with people 'whose clothing differed conspicuously from the well-dressed morning congregations'. Archibald Tait died at Addington Palace in 1882 and was buried in the parish churchyard there. An ornate memorial to him in polychrome marble stands in the north-east transept at Canterbury. The inscription reads: 'A great archbishop, just, discerning, dignified, statesmanlike; wise to know the time and resolute to redeem it'.

Tait's successor as archbishop was Edward White Benson, an autocratic and driven man who was born in Birmingham in 1829 and educated at King Edward's School and Cambridge University. He began his career as a teacher at Rugby School before being ordained priest in 1857 and becoming the first headmaster of Wellington College two years later. Subsequent appointments included the chancellorship of Lincoln and the bishopric of the newly created diocese of Truro, where he began work on the new cathedral, followed by his installation as Archbishop of Canterbury in 1883. Benson is best remembered in Cornwall for his introduction of the service of nine lessons and carols, first performed in Truro Cathedral on Christmas Eve 1880.

The most significant issue during his time in office at Canterbury was the trial of Edward King, the Bishop of Lincoln, who was charged in 1888 with tolerating six ritual offences under the Public Worship Regulation Act. Benson managed to avoid King's case coming before a lay tribunal by hearing it in his own archiepiscopal court (which had sat only once since the Reformation). In his judgement, known as the Lincoln Judgement, the Archbishop found King guilty on two counts, instructing him to keep his hands clearly visible when consecrating the elements at Holy Communion. In this way people could be assured that the bread and wine were not being covertly transformed into the body and blood of Christ. But the use of candles on the altar was specifically approved by Benson in his judgement, as also were the signing of the cross and the mixing of the water and the wine.

Edward White Benson died in October 1896 while staying with William Gladstone at his home in Wales. He was the first Archbishop of Canterbury to be buried in the cathedral since Reginald Pole in 1558 – and he was also the last. His splendid tomb is sited in St Augustine's Chapel beneath the north-west tower.

THE EARLY 20ᵀᴴ CENTURY ARCHBISHOPS: 1896–1942

Following Edward White Benson's death in 1896, the archiepiscopal throne was occupied by Frederick Temple. He was seventy-six years old and losing his sight. Temple was born in 1821 on the Ionian island of Santa Maura and educated at Blundell's School and Oxford University. He was ordained in 1846 and appointed chaplain-in-ordinary to Queen Victoria ten years later. In 1858, he became headmaster of Rugby School where he was rather more successful than Archibald Tait had been a decade earlier. He strengthened the school's reputation in the humanities, nurtured the sciences and beefed up the sports. His sermons to the boys were characterised by their emphasis on the Victorian public-school virtues of loyalty, faith and duty. They reflected Temple's own character: rugged, austere and even abrupt on the surface but deeply compassionate within.

It was early in Temple's time at Rugby that Charles Darwin's *Origin of Species* was published (in 1859) and the famous confrontation between Thomas Huxley and Bishop Samuel Wilberforce took place at Oxford. Temple's long-standing interest in science drew him into the debate about the origins of life, and he immediately accepted the explanatory power of Darwin's ideas. In 1884 he gave the Bampton Lectures at Oxford, an annual series of talks on Christian theology by distinguished speakers. Addressing the relationship between religion and science, Temple concluded that: 'the doctrine of evolution is in no sense whatever antagonistic to the teachings of religion'.

Politically close to William Gladstone and the Liberal party, Temple accepted the bishopric of Exeter in 1869, having earlier turned down the deanship of Durham. The appointment raised a storm of protest in conservative quarters, but Temple won his critics round with his diligence (his typical working day was fourteen or fifteen hours), and in 1885 he was promoted from Exeter to the diocese of London where he was closely associated with the temperance movement. As his sight deteriorated with advancing age, Temple offered his resignation; but he was persuaded not only to change his mind about remaining as Bishop of London but also, following Edward Benson's sudden death in 1896, to accept preferment to Canterbury.

RIGHT: Funeral cortège of Queen Victoria, 1901

It fell to Temple as archbishop to speak for the Church of England at the start of the 20th century, and he used the occasion to call for unity in a Church that was, he believed, still riven with damaging divisions between its Anglo-Catholic and its low-church factions. Without a more charitable temper, he thought, the Church would fail in its mission to evangelise the nation. In 1897 Temple convened the fourth Lambeth Conference, and in August 1902 he crowned King Edward VII and Queen Alexandra, but the strain of office was now taking its toll. As he was speaking in the House of Lords in December 1902, he collapsed. Although he was able to finish his speech, he never fully recovered and died three weeks later. An elaborate memorial was erected in the Corona at Canterbury opposite the tomb of the last Roman Catholic archbishop, Reginald Pole.

Frederick Temple's successor, Randall Davidson, was born to Scottish Presbyterian parents in 1848 and educated at Harrow and Oxford. In his final year at school, he was involved in a shooting accident that left a number of pellets embedded in his lower back, weakening some abdominal muscles. The resultant hernia, which caused Davidson to wear a truss throughout his life, occasionally dropped – especially, he once remarked, when he was in the pulpit.

From early in his career, Davidson moved in elevated circles. He was chaplain to Archbishop Tait (whose daughter, Edith, he married) and later to Archbishop Benson. Favoured by Queen Victoria, he was appointed Dean of Windsor at the age of thirty-six, and it was only with the Queen's reluctant consent that he was elevated to the episcopacy in 1891 as Bishop of Rochester. Then came the bishopric of Winchester in 1895, where he played a major part in orchestrating the funeral ceremonies for Queen Victoria in 1901, and finally promotion to Canterbury in 1903. Davidson remained in the office for twenty-five years – the longest since the Reformation – and when he resigned in 1928, he was the first Archbishop of Canterbury to do so voluntarily. His decision to retire may have been precipitated by his reluctance to face another exhausting Lambeth Conference, for he had already presided over two (in 1908 and 1920) and he had attended five of the first six.

Davidson may also have been worn down by the continuing controversy in the Church of England over the *Book of Common Prayer*. A royal commission report in 1906 had set in train a move to revise the 1662 edition – a lengthy process, as it turned out, that spanned the whole of Davidson's time as Archbishop. The new version was finally approved by the newly created Church Assembly in 1927 but still had to pass through parliament. It was accepted by the House of Lords, but was narrowly defeated in the Commons. The same thing happened in the following year. Notwithstanding the lack of parliamentary approval, the 1928 version was eventually authorised for use, but parishes were free to decide whether or not to do so. It was in the midst of the resultant confusion that Davidson chose to retire. He remained in the House of Lords as Lord Davidson of Lambeth and, on his death in 1930, he was buried in the cloister garth at Canterbury. A memorial to him stands in the Trinity Chapel.

Randall Davidson was succeeded by Cosmo Gordon Lang, a Scottish son of the manse who achieved the unprecedented feat of becoming Archbishop of York in 1908 only eighteen years after his ordination as priest. Lang was born in 1864 and educated at the Universities of Glasgow and Oxford. In the 1890s he was a curate in Leeds, living in a derelict pub in a run-down part of the city where many of his neighbours were prostitutes. After a spell as Dean of Magdalen College, Oxford, Lang became vicar of Portsea, a dockside parish in Portsmouth. While there, he was commanded to preach to Queen Victoria at Osborne House on the Isle of Wight and made such an impression that he became a regular visitor to the royal household.

In 1901 Lang was consecrated Bishop of Stepney, and in 1908 he was nominated to the archbishopric of York by Herbert Asquith – an extraordinary preferment for a suffragan who was still only forty-four. At York, Lang was known for his mildly Anglo-Catholic stance on Church issues and for his moderate conservatism on political matters. He believed that the Great War was morally just – a viewpoint that elicited what he described as 'a hail of denunciation' through the post – and he even spoke out against excessive anti-German propaganda. By now a trusted confidant of the royal family, Lang was particularly close to King George V, whose pioneering Christmas broadcasts he helped to draft.

Lang's time as Archbishop of Canterbury between 1928 and 1942 inevitably brought him into the public spotlight over a number of high-profile issues. He resolved the 1928 stalemate over the *Book of Common Prayer* by allowing it to be used with local parochial approval; he presided over the Lambeth Conference in 1930 that gave qualified sanction to the use of birth control by married couples, and he worked hard for the cause of international ecumenism.

By now, however, Lang's earlier image as one concerned with the plight of the poor had largely dissipated as he came increasingly to be seen as an establishment figure. His closeness to the royal family was, however, clouded by the abdication crisis of 1936, for he disapproved of the Prince of Wales's relationship with Wallis Simpson and tried to prevent the marriage from taking place. Two days after the abdication, Lang broadcast a speech in which he accused the former king of flouting the principles of Christian marriage. The speech, which he unwisely wrote without consulting anyone, was heavily criticised for its lack of charity, appearing to many as if the Archbishop was kicking a man who was already down. Lang later spoke of his immense relief that the matter was now over, since he hadn't been sure he could have gone through with the coronation. But he had no qualms about crowning King George VI in May 1937 – the first such ceremony to be broadcast and filmed. The footage seemed to indicate that he needed two or three attempts before positioning the crown correctly on the King's head.

The prospect of a long war, followed by yet another Lambeth Conference, had now become obstacles too far for Cosmo Gordon Lang, and in November 1941 he informed Winston Churchill of his intention to retire. His last official act, in March 1942, was the confirmation of the young Princess Elizabeth. Upon retirement, he was ennobled as Baron Lang of Lambeth and given a large rent-free house on Kew Green. In December 1945, he collapsed as he walked to Kew Garden station and died on the way to hospital. His ashes were interred in St Stephen's Chapel in Canterbury Cathedral.

WAR AND THE COLD WAR: 1942–1974

Although it is not in the gift of an archbishop to nominate his successor, Cosmo Gordon Lang's preferred candidate, William Temple, did follow him into the office. The son of Archbishop Frederick Temple, he is widely seen as one of the most able and admired Anglican bishops of the 20th century in spite of the tragically short time he had as Archbishop of Canterbury. Popularly known as 'the people's Archbishop', Temple was born in 1881 while his father was Bishop of Exeter, and his education at Rugby and Oxford followed a conventional path for those destined for high office in the Church of England. His wide abilities were recognised at Oxford where he obtained a double first in Classics and was president of the Union. Ordained priest in December 1909, Temple was headmaster of Repton School from 1910 to 1914; later he was consecrated Bishop of Manchester in 1921 and appointed Archbishop of York in 1929. In 1932 he gave the prestigious Gifford Lectures at Glasgow University on the theme of nature, man and God. He used the talks to counter the fashionable Marxist doctrines of the day with an alternative vision of Christian socialism.

Temple was appointed Archbishop of Canterbury in 1942, the year in which he published his highly influential book *Christianity and the Social Order*. The book – which sought to justify the Church's engagement in political action – had its roots in Temple's lasting commitment to social and educational reform. In spite of his privileged background and ease in socially elevated circles, Temple readily moved beyond his comfort zone in the cause of ecumenism and social justice. He was influential in the formation of the British and World Councils of Churches and was a co-founder of the Council of Christians and Jews. Moved by the plight of European Jews during the Second World War, Temple angered many Quakers and other pacifists by pointedly refusing to condemn the allied carpet-bombing of Nazi Germany.

As the War progressed, there was a mood of expectancy in the Church of England that Temple would use the authority of his office to press for a fairer and more civilised society in post-war Britain, but it was not to be. Beset by a severe form of gout from a young age, he succumbed to complications of the disease and died in October 1944 at the age of only sixty-three – the last Archbishop (to date) to have died in office. His ashes were buried close to those of his father in the cloister garth at Canterbury.

William Temple was succeeded by Geoffrey Fisher, whose early life and career – like Temple's – seemed destined to take him to the very top of the tree. Born in 1887 into a family with a long history of Anglican ministry, he was educated at Marlborough and Oxford before being ordained priest in 1913. In the following year, he succeeded Temple as headmaster of Repton School where his pupils included Michael Ramsey, who was later to follow him as Archbishop of Canterbury. On leaving Repton in 1932, Fisher was consecrated Bishop of Chester and, seven years later, appointed Bishop of London. In both positions, he represented a solidly middle-of-the-road Anglicanism laced with courtesy, skill and determination.

ABOVE: **Geoffrey Fisher,** artist unknown

RIGHT: **Michael Ramsey,** by George Bruce

When the archbishopric of Canterbury suddenly became vacant in 1944, many in the Church of England expected George Bell – the Bishop of Chichester and a former Dean of Canterbury – to be appointed, but any such expectations were dashed. Bell was a high-profile opponent of the indiscriminate bombing of Germany by allied forces, and it may have been this that turned the prime minister, Winston Churchill, against him. In the event, Fisher was appointed, holding office for the remainder of the war and into the troubled post-war years of rationing and mutual suspicion between the West and the Soviet bloc.

As Archbishop, Fisher was seen as an austere and conservative figure who never attained the popularity that William Temple had enjoyed. Instinctively mistrustful of change and innovation, he was perpetually at loggerheads with the Dean of Canterbury, Hewlett Johnson, whose maverick behaviour he never managed to curb. Ecclesiastically, Fisher's principal achievement – and his greatest satisfaction – was the work he did behind the scenes on revising the canon law of the Church of England, parts of which had remained unchanged for more than three hundred years. The revisions finally came into effect in 1969.

Fisher was, however, far from a shrinking violet: indeed, he was (with Hewlett Johnson) one of the most recognisable public figures in post-war Britain. His image was beamed into thousands of households at the coronation of Queen Elizabeth II in 1953 – only the second occasion on which an Archbishop of Canterbury had been filmed crowning the monarch – and he also became the first archbishop since 1397 to meet the Pope when he visited John XXIII in Jerusalem in 1960. Fisher's opinions sometimes made headline news, such as when he suggested – at a time of heightened fear about the possibility of outright nuclear war – that it may be within the providence of God that the human race should destroy itself in this way. The worst the bomb could do, he was reported to have said, would be to sweep vast numbers of people from this world into the next.

Geoffrey Fisher retired in 1961, but not before advising the prime minister, Harold Macmillan, that he did not consider his erstwhile pupil at Repton School, Michael Ramsey, to be the right choice as his successor. Ramsey was, Fisher said, a theologian, a scholar and a man of prayer and therefore entirely unsuitable to be an archbishop. 'Thank you, your Grace, for your kind advice', Macmillan replied. 'You may have been Dr Ramsey's headmaster but you are not going to be mine'. He added, by way of explanation, that 'I thought we had had enough of Martha and it was time for some Mary'. Michael Ramsey was duly enthroned in June 1961 as the one-hundredth Archbishop of Canterbury.

ABOVE: Geoffrey Fisher crowns Queen Elizabeth II in 1953

The family into which Ramsey was born in 1904 was talented but disparate. His mother was a socialist and a suffragist; his father was a Congregationalist deacon, and his older brother, Frank, was a brilliant economist of atheistic persuasions who died young. Ramsey was educated at Repton School and Cambridge, where he encountered a range of Christian traditions. He was ordained priest in 1928 and his early ministry took him to Liverpool, Boston (Lincolnshire) and Cambridge before his appointment as Professor of Divinity at Durham University. Ramsey was consecrated Bishop of Durham in 1952 and was appointed Archbishop of York in 1956 and of Canterbury in 1961.

As archbishop, Ramsey was a large and instantly recognisable figure, entirely lacking in pomposity and always ready to engage with anyone who wanted to talk to him, particularly young people and students. An Anglo-Catholic with non-conformist sympathies, he had a broad religious outlook tempered by a wariness of liberal fads and fashions. He was initially hostile (as were most senior Anglicans) towards John Robinson's ground-breaking book *Honest to God* in 1963, and he was uneasy about the movement for women's ordination in the Church of England, even though he saw no fundamental theological objections to it. In most areas of his ministry, however, Ramsey reached out enthusiastically and effectively to other traditions and new ideas. In 1966 he met Pope Paul VI in Rome, an event that he described as 'the highlight of my life', and he got on well with the patriarchs whom he met from the Eastern Orthodox Churches. He was deeply disappointed when proposals for a union between the Church of England and the Methodist Church were scuppered at the last minute by the General Synod in 1972.

Politically, Ramsey distanced himself from the conservatism of many of his immediate predecessors. He had little enthusiasm for the established status of the Anglican Church and he was ill at ease with royalty. He caused outrage in some quarters in 1967 by supporting the decriminalisation of homosexual acts among consenting adults and he upset conservatives in the Church by arguing that, if the government deemed it practical, it would be right to use British troops to overthrow the white minority regime of Ian Smith in what was then Rhodesia. Ramsey also spoke out against the apartheid policies of John Vorster in South Africa and the dictatorship of Augusto Pinochet in Chile.

Michael Ramsey retired in 1974 and died at Oxford in April 1988. His ashes are buried in the cloister garth at Canterbury, close to those of Frederick and William Temple. The inscription on the memorial stone reads: 'The Glory of God is the living man, and the life of man is the vision of God'.

BREAKING THE MOULD: 1974–2012

Michael Ramsey's successor, Donald Coggan, had a far less promising start in life than many of his predecessors, and there was nothing in it to indicate the ecclesiastical heights that he would eventually reach. Born in 1909 to a north London businessman, Coggan had a sickly childhood and was taught at home for a number of years before entering the Merchant Taylors School in Charterhouse Square. He secured a place at Cambridge University and graduated with a double first in oriental languages. Coggan's early career brought him teaching appointments at Manchester University, Wycliffe College in Toronto and the London College of Divinity. Ordained priest in 1935, he was consecrated Bishop of Bradford in 1956, and he succeeded Michael Ramsey as Archbishop of York in 1961. He later followed Ramsey to Canterbury in 1974 at the age of sixty-five.

Though lacking his predecessor's charisma and physical presence, Coggan was a conscientious pastor, a careful administrator and an evangelical who believed that the Church was at its best when preaching the Christian gospel to those outside its walls. He has been described as perhaps the first Archbishop of Canterbury to direct his words as much to those untouched by Christianity as to those already committed to it. His 'Call to the Nation' in 1975, setting out his vision of a society transformed by social compassion, drew a positive response even if – like other similar initiatives from churchmen and politicians – it achieved little of lasting value.

As Archbishop, Coggan strongly supported the ordination of women, which he lived to see happen in the Church of England in 1994, and he was active in Bible societies in America and elsewhere. The Lord Coggan Memorial Fund, which he founded after his retirement, was controversially involved in the supply of bibles to children in Russia. Aside from his duties as archbishop, Coggan was a prolific writer and a generous host. He is credited with saying that 'the art of hospitality is to make guests feel at home when you wish they really were'. He retired in 1980 and died in Winchester ten years later. Following a memorial service in Winchester Cathedral, his ashes were buried in the cloister garth at Canterbury.

Donald Coggan's successor, Robert Runcie, was another who broke the mould in which archbishops of Canterbury had traditionally been formed. Born into a largely non-religious family in Lancashire in 1921, Runcie was educated at the Merchant Taylors School in Crosby and Oxford University. Serving as a tank commander with the Scots Guards in the Second World War, he was awarded the Military Cross for two feats of bravery in March 1945, and shortly afterwards he was among the first British troops to enter the Bergen-Belsen concentration camp. After the War, Runcie returned to Oxford, gaining a first in Greats (Greek and Roman history) and making an initial acquaintance with Margaret Roberts – later to become his nemesis as prime minister at the time of the Falklands' conflict.

Runcie was ordained priest in 1950 and served as a curate in Newcastle before moving to Cambridge in 1956 as Dean of Trinity Hall. He spent ten years as principal of Cuddesdon

RIGHT: Clockwise from left: George Carey, by June Mendoza; Donald Coggan, by Elizabeth Narraway; Robert Runcie, by David Poole

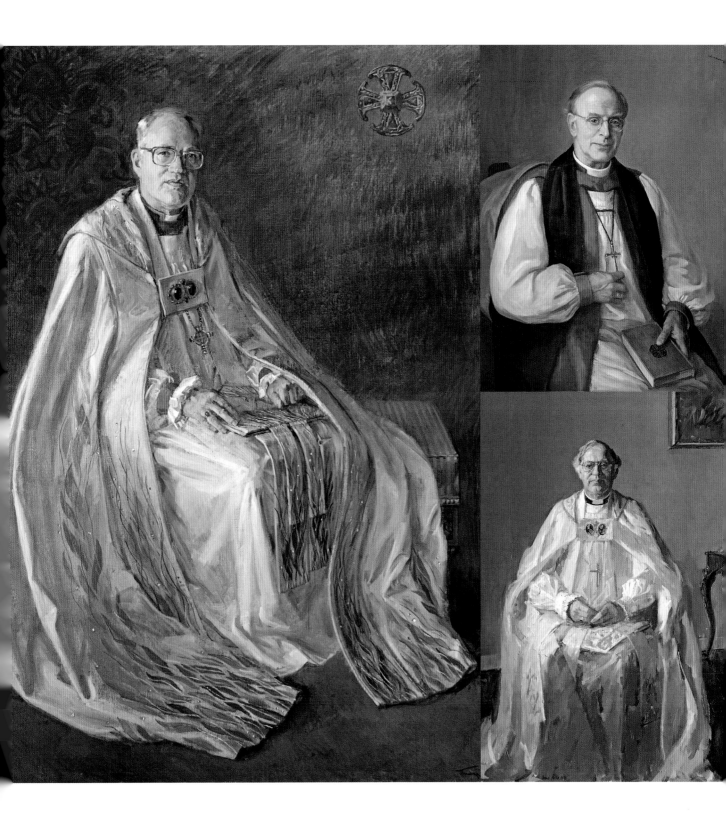

College before his installation as Bishop of St Albans in 1970 and Archbishop of Canterbury ten years later. Thereafter, Runcie was frequently in the spotlight of controversy as the Church of England repeatedly found itself on the front line of opposition to the Conservative government. In 1982 the prime minister, Margaret Thatcher, was said by her husband to have 'spitted blood' over the sermon preached by Runcie in St Paul's Cathedral to mark the end of the Falkland's conflict. In 1985, the publication of *Faith in the City* – a Church of England response to the inner-city rioting that had erupted episodically in Liverpool and Birmingham – was dismissed by a prominent member of Thatcher's cabinet as 'pure Marxist theology'. On many social issues – especially those concerned with poverty and deprivation – the Anglican episcopacy under Runcie frequently made headline news.

A brief respite from controversy came in 1981 when Runcie officiated at the wedding of Prince Charles and Lady Diana Spencer, but in the following year he faced an angry backlash from die-hard Protestants in his native Merseyside over the visit to Britain of Pope John Paul II. He also incurred the wrath of conservative Anglicans over his strong support for the ordination of women in the Church of England, while from the liberal end of the spectrum he was criticised for upholding the Church's traditional views on homosexuality – even though he admitted that he had probably consecrated bishops who were in same-sex relationships. Such attacks could be dismissed as part of the job, but the anguish that Runcie suffered through the ordeal of Terry Waite was deeply and painfully personal. In 1980 Waite was appointed by Runcie as special envoy to the worldwide Anglican Communion, and seven years later he was taken hostage in Beirut by an Islamic jihadi organisation. Waite remained in captivity for almost five years, during which time his plight became increasingly forgotten by the public; he was finally released in November 1991, to the unconstrained relief and joy of the recently retired Archbishop.

Robert Runcie and his wife Rosalind lived in St Albans during the ten years of his retirement. He died in January 2000 and was buried in the grounds of St Albans Cathedral. His successor, George Carey, broke the traditional primate's mould even more decisively than either Coggan or Runcie by being the first Archbishop of Canterbury since Simon Sudbury in the 14th century not to have been educated at either Oxford or Cambridge. Carey left school at the age of fifteen and worked as an office boy before doing national service in the RAF. Following a profoundly moving conversion experience at the age of seventeen, he began to prepare himself for ordination and, after parish work and appointments at various theological colleges, he became Bishop of Bath and Wells in 1987. He was enthroned as Archbishop of Canterbury in 1991. Identified quite strongly with the evangelical wing of the Church of England, Carey was not well known among the general public, and his appointment was seen by many at the time as a surprising choice.

As Archbishop, Carey supported the ordination of women but he strongly opposed any dilution of the Church's official line on homosexuality, especially among the clergy. It was an issue that over-shadowed the 1998 Lambeth Conference, which Carey convened and chaired. He had hoped that the Conference's rejection of homosexual practices as being 'incompatible with scripture' would be the end of the matter. However, it turned out otherwise, for questions of human sexuality soon escalated into a crisis that was to haunt the Anglican Communion in the years that followed.

Carey's time as Archbishop was noted for his initiation of a 'Decade of Evangelism' in the Church of England, but his religious concerns extended beyond the confines of the Christian faith. Although he tried, with some success, to reach out to Islam, he was criticised when he

took moderate Muslims to task for failing to see the dangers posed by extremists. He worried about the scale of immigration into Britain, arguing that the diverse faiths and values of many immigrants were muddying the notion of 'Britishness', especially where religion was concerned. At the same time, Carey made a point of supporting Christians who were suffering oppression and discrimination throughout the world, and he called on the government to 'welcome Christian refugees [to Britain] and give them priority as asylum seekers'.

Following his retirement in October 2002, Carey continued to maintain a high public profile, commenting more outspokenly than his retired predecessors had done on a range of issues including same-sex relationships, the Church of England's investments in the arms industry, and the dangers of uncontrolled immigration. His public pronouncements on these matters led to accusations of meddling in things that he should have left behind and, worse, of disloyalty to his successor. When he said in 2006 that he was 'ashamed to be an Anglican' following the General Synod's decision to withdraw its investments from companies profiting from Israel's occupation of Palestinian territories, he received critical correspondence from several Anglican communities around the world, but he remained undeterred by them.

George Carey's successor, Rowan Williams, further broke the mould by being the first Archbishop of Canterbury since the Reformation to be appointed from outside the Church of England: before his appointment in 2002, he was Archbishop of the Church of Wales. Born in 1950 into a Welsh-speaking family in Swansea, Williams read theology at Cambridge and graduated from Oxford with a doctorate in 1975. He was ordained priest in 1978, and after serving a curacy at Cambridge, he was appointed Lady Margaret Professor of Divinity at Oxford at the age of only thirty-six. Williams was consecrated Bishop of Monmouth in 1992 and Archbishop of Wales in 1999 before his enthronement at Canterbury in 2003.

Williams's appointment was widely seen as a counter-balance to Carey's uncomplicated evangelicalism. A scholar of dazzlingly diverse talents, Williams had far too subtle an understanding of the Christian faith for his views to be encapsulated in a few simple soundbites. However, while his academic style of speaking and writing was counted a virtue by many, it sometimes handicapped him in an age when communications of more than a few sentences were not in fashion. Moreover, the nuances of some of Williams's personal convictions made it difficult for him at times to address the concerns of those who took a more fundamentalist line. Thus, while he saw no scriptural objections to the consecration of women bishops and was prepared to reinterpret the biblical injunctions against homosexuality, he was all too aware of the widespread objections that such departures from the traditional teaching of the Church might arouse – not only in Britain but also in Africa, the Americas, Australia and elsewhere.

Such tensions might have been eased by acknowledging the ultimate inevitability of schism within the Anglican Communion, but to Williams that would have been a betrayal of his deepest beliefs about the Church. As a result, he never let up in his attempts to hold the Communion together in the face of the theological and moral pressures welling up within it. His efforts in this regard were not without success, for Williams was able to hand over to his successor a confederation of churches that had largely avoided the fragmentation some had feared, especially in the wake of the Lambeth Conference in 2008 that became mired yet again in issues of human sexuality. His critics, however, saw his efforts as little more than a short-term fix, secured only by a failure to confront head-on the depth and diversity of views within the communion.

Intellectually, Williams was one of the most brilliant polymaths ever to occupy the throne of St Augustine. Theologian, poet, linguist, scholar, bard – there seemed to be no area of literary creativity in which he could not shine. He was also an archbishop of palpable spirituality and prayerfulness. Yet Williams's popular image, as a bearded, other-worldly prophet of old, belied his incisive engagements with the great social and political controversies of his day. The issues on which he spoke could scarcely have been more important: Islamic Sharia law, the market state, taxation, social security, terrorism, the abuse of children within the Church and much else besides. Throughout his period in office, Williams engaged in a breathtaking agenda of public discourse that seemed, finally, to exhaust him and that may have been instrumental in his decision to retire after ten gruelling years as archbishop.

Rowan Williams stepped down from office at the end of 2012 and took up the position of Master of Magdalene College, Cambridge. He was ennobled as Baron Williams of Oystermouth in 2013, enabling him to continue to speak in the House of Lords on the great issues of the day.

Rowan Williams was succeeded by Justin Welby, who was enthroned as Archbishop of Canterbury in March 2013.

RIGHT: Justin Welby, 105th Archbishop of Canterbury and the most senior bishop in the Church of England